C-2187 CAREER EXAMINATION SERIES

*This is your
PASSBOOK for...*

Systems Programmer

*Test Preparation Study Guide
Questions & Answers*

COPYRIGHT NOTICE

This book is SOLELY intended for, is sold ONLY to, and its use is RESTRICTED to individual, bona fide applicants or candidates who qualify by virtue of having seriously filed applications for appropriate license, certificate, professional and/or promotional advancement, higher school matriculation, scholarship, or other legitimate requirements of education and/or governmental authorities.

This book is NOT intended for use, class instruction, tutoring, training, duplication, copying, reprinting, excerption, or adaptation, etc., by:

1) Other publishers
2) Proprietors and/or Instructors of "Coaching" and/or Preparatory Courses
3) Personnel and/or Training Divisions of commercial, industrial, and governmental organizations
4) Schools, colleges, or universities and/or their departments and staffs, including teachers and other personnel
5) Testing Agencies or Bureaus
6) Study groups which seek by the purchase of a single volume to copy and/or duplicate and/or adapt this material for use by the group as a whole without having purchased individual volumes for each of the members of the group
7) Et al.

Such persons would be in violation of appropriate Federal and State statutes.

PROVISION OF LICENSING AGREEMENTS – Recognized educational, commercial, industrial, and governmental institutions and organizations, and others legitimately engaged in educational pursuits, including training, testing, and measurement activities, may address request for a licensing agreement to the copyright owners, who will determine whether, and under what conditions, including fees and charges, the materials in this book may be used them. In other words, a licensing facility exists for the legitimate use of the material in this book on other than an individual basis. However, it is asseverated and affirmed here that the material in this book CANNOT be used without the receipt of the express permission of such a licensing agreement from the Publishers. Inquiries re licensing should be addressed to the company, attention rights and permissions department.

All rights reserved, including the right of reproduction in whole or in part, in any form or by any means, electronic or mechanical, including photocopying, recording, or by any information storage and retrieval system, without permission in writing from the Publisher.

Copyright © 2025 by
National Learning Corporation

212 Michael Drive, Syosset, NY 11791
(516) 921-8888 • www.passbooks.com
E-mail: info@passbooks.com

PASSBOOK® SERIES

THE *PASSBOOK® SERIES* has been created to prepare applicants and candidates for the ultimate academic battlefield – the examination room.

At some time in our lives, each and every one of us may be required to take an examination – for validation, matriculation, admission, qualification, registration, certification, or licensure.

Based on the assumption that every applicant or candidate has met the basic formal educational standards, has taken the required number of courses, and read the necessary texts, the *PASSBOOK® SERIES* furnishes the one special preparation which may assure passing with confidence, instead of failing with insecurity. Examination questions – together with answers – are furnished as the basic vehicle for study so that the mysteries of the examination and its compounding difficulties may be eliminated or diminished by a sure method.

This book is meant to help you pass your examination provided that you qualify and are serious in your objective.

The entire field is reviewed through the huge store of content information which is succinctly presented through a provocative and challenging approach – the question-and-answer method.

A climate of success is established by furnishing the correct answers at the end of each test.

You soon learn to recognize types of questions, forms of questions, and patterns of questioning. You may even begin to anticipate expected outcomes.

You perceive that many questions are repeated or adapted so that you can gain acute insights, which may enable you to score many sure points.

You learn how to confront new questions, or types of questions, and to attack them confidently and work out the correct answers.

You note objectives and emphases, and recognize pitfalls and dangers, so that you may make positive educational adjustments.

Moreover, you are kept fully informed in relation to new concepts, methods, practices, and directions in the field.

You discover that you are actually taking the examination all the time: you are preparing for the examination by "taking" an examination, not by reading extraneous and/or supererogatory textbooks.

In short, this PASSBOOK®, used directedly, should be an important factor in helping you to pass your test.

SYSTEMS PROGRAMMER

DUTIES
Maintains a data processing operating system through the coordination of a programming and systems staff of a data processing department. Has full responsibility for all the activities of programming and systems pertaining to the modifications and improvements of hardware and software capabilities of the operating system.

As a Systems Programmer, you would perform systems programming and implement, maintain and manage an agency's hardware and systems software environment or major component of it. You would write, install and modify all types of systems software; evaluate new systems software offered by vendors; and act as liaison with other agency information technology professionals and vendors. You may analyze production problems to determine if they are caused by hardware and/or software malfunctions or may monitor systems for performance and capacity planning. You may supervise one or more lower-level information technology specialists and/or computer operations staff performing systems maintenance and development-related activities. Perform related work as required.

SCOPE OF THE EXAMINATION
The written test will cover knowledge, skills and/or abilities in such areas as:

1. Systems programming, operating systems, and associated equipment;
2. Systems analysis and design;
3. Use of a pseudo assembly language;
4. Project management fundamentals;
5. Logical reasoning using flowcharts; and
6. Preparing written material.

HOW TO TAKE A TEST

I. YOU MUST PASS AN EXAMINATION

A. WHAT EVERY CANDIDATE SHOULD KNOW

Examination applicants often ask us for help in preparing for the written test. What can I study in advance? What kinds of questions will be asked? How will the test be given? How will the papers be graded?

As an applicant for a civil service examination, you may be wondering about some of these things. Our purpose here is to suggest effective methods of advance study and to describe civil service examinations.

Your chances for success on this examination can be increased if you know how to prepare. Those "pre-examination jitters" can be reduced if you know what to expect. You can even experience an adventure in good citizenship if you know why civil service exams are given.

B. WHY ARE CIVIL SERVICE EXAMINATIONS GIVEN?

Civil service examinations are important to you in two ways. As a citizen, you want public jobs filled by employees who know how to do their work. As a job seeker, you want a fair chance to compete for that job on an equal footing with other candidates. The best-known means of accomplishing this two-fold goal is the competitive examination.

Exams are widely publicized throughout the nation. They may be administered for jobs in federal, state, city, municipal, town or village governments or agencies.

Any citizen may apply, with some limitations, such as the age or residence of applicants. Your experience and education may be reviewed to see whether you meet the requirements for the particular examination. When these requirements exist, they are reasonable and applied consistently to all applicants. Thus, a competitive examination may cause you some uneasiness now, but it is your privilege and safeguard.

C. HOW ARE CIVIL SERVICE EXAMS DEVELOPED?

Examinations are carefully written by trained technicians who are specialists in the field known as "psychological measurement," in consultation with recognized authorities in the field of work that the test will cover. These experts recommend the subject matter areas or skills to be tested; only those knowledges or skills important to your success on the job are included. The most reliable books and source materials available are used as references. Together, the experts and technicians judge the difficulty level of the questions.

Test technicians know how to phrase questions so that the problem is clearly stated. Their ethics do not permit "trick" or "catch" questions. Questions may have been tried out on sample groups, or subjected to statistical analysis, to determine their usefulness.

Written tests are often used in combination with performance tests, ratings of training and experience, and oral interviews. All of these measures combine to form the best-known means of finding the right person for the right job.

II. HOW TO PASS THE WRITTEN TEST

A. NATURE OF THE EXAMINATION

To prepare intelligently for civil service examinations, you should know how they differ from school examinations you have taken. In school you were assigned certain definite pages to read or subjects to cover. The examination questions were quite detailed and usually emphasized memory. Civil service exams, on the other hand, try to discover your present ability to perform the duties of a position, plus your potentiality to learn these duties. In other words, a civil service exam attempts to predict how successful you will be. Questions cover such a broad area that they cannot be as minute and detailed as school exam questions.

In the public service similar kinds of work, or positions, are grouped together in one "class." This process is known as *position-classification*. All the positions in a class are paid according to the salary range for that class. One class title covers all of these positions, and they are all tested by the same examination.

B. FOUR BASIC STEPS

1) Study the announcement

How, then, can you know what subjects to study? Our best answer is: "Learn as much as possible about the class of positions for which you've applied." The exam will test the knowledge, skills and abilities needed to do the work.

Your most valuable source of information about the position you want is the official exam announcement. This announcement lists the training and experience qualifications. Check these standards and apply only if you come reasonably close to meeting them.

The brief description of the position in the examination announcement offers some clues to the subjects which will be tested. Think about the job itself. Review the duties in your mind. Can you perform them, or are there some in which you are rusty? Fill in the blank spots in your preparation.

Many jurisdictions preview the written test in the exam announcement by including a section called "Knowledge and Abilities Required," "Scope of the Examination," or some similar heading. Here you will find out specifically what fields will be tested.

2) Review your own background

Once you learn in general what the position is all about, and what you need to know to do the work, ask yourself which subjects you already know fairly well and which need improvement. You may wonder whether to concentrate on improving your strong areas or on building some background in your fields of weakness. When the announcement has specified "some knowledge" or "considerable knowledge," or has used adjectives like "beginning principles of..." or "advanced ... methods," you can get a clue as to the number and difficulty of questions to be asked in any given field. More questions, and hence broader coverage, would be included for those subjects which are more important in the work. Now weigh your strengths and weaknesses against the job requirements and prepare accordingly.

3) Determine the level of the position

Another way to tell how intensively you should prepare is to understand the level of the job for which you are applying. Is it the entering level? In other words, is this the position in which beginners in a field of work are hired? Or is it an intermediate or advanced level? Sometimes this is indicated by such words as "Junior" or "Senior" in the class title. Other jurisdictions use Roman numerals to designate the level – Clerk I, Clerk II, for example. The word "Supervisor" sometimes appears in the title. If the level is not indicated by the title, check the description of duties. Will you be working under very close supervision, or will you have responsibility for independent decisions in this work?

4) Choose appropriate study materials

Now that you know the subjects to be examined and the relative amount of each subject to be covered, you can choose suitable study materials. For beginning level jobs, or even advanced ones, if you have a pronounced weakness in some aspect of your training, read a modern, standard textbook in that field. Be sure it is up to date and has general coverage. Such books are normally available at your library, and the librarian will be glad to help you locate one. For entry-level positions, questions of appropriate difficulty are chosen – neither highly advanced questions, nor those too simple. Such questions require careful thought but not advanced training.

If the position for which you are applying is technical or advanced, you will read more advanced, specialized material. If you are already familiar with the basic principles of your field, elementary textbooks would waste your time. Concentrate on advanced textbooks and technical periodicals. Think through the concepts and review difficult problems in your field.

These are all general sources. You can get more ideas on your own initiative, following these leads. For example, training manuals and publications of the government agency which employs workers in your field can be useful, particularly for technical and professional positions. A letter or visit to the government department involved may result in more specific study suggestions, and certainly will provide you with a more definite idea of the exact nature of the position you are seeking.

III. KINDS OF TESTS

Tests are used for purposes other than measuring knowledge and ability to perform specified duties. For some positions, it is equally important to test ability to make adjustments to new situations or to profit from training. In others, basic mental abilities not dependent on information are essential. Questions which test these things may not appear as pertinent to the duties of the position as those which test for knowledge and information. Yet they are often highly important parts of a fair examination. For very general questions, it is almost impossible to help you direct your study efforts. What we can do is to point out some of the more common of these general abilities needed in public service positions and describe some typical questions.

1) General information

Broad, general information has been found useful for predicting job success in some kinds of work. This is tested in a variety of ways, from vocabulary lists to questions about current events. Basic background in some field of work, such as sociology or economics, may be sampled in a group of questions. Often these are principles which have become familiar to most persons through exposure rather than through formal training. It is difficult to advise you how to study for these questions; being alert to the world around you is our best suggestion.

2) Verbal ability

An example of an ability needed in many positions is verbal or language ability. Verbal ability is, in brief, the ability to use and understand words. Vocabulary and grammar tests are typical measures of this ability. Reading comprehension or paragraph interpretation questions are common in many kinds of civil service tests. You are given a paragraph of written material and asked to find its central meaning.

3) Numerical ability

Number skills can be tested by the familiar arithmetic problem, by checking paired lists of numbers to see which are alike and which are different, or by interpreting charts and graphs. In the latter test, a graph may be printed in the test booklet which you are asked to use as the basis for answering questions.

4) Observation

A popular test for law-enforcement positions is the observation test. A picture is shown to you for several minutes, then taken away. Questions about the picture test your ability to observe both details and larger elements.

5) Following directions

In many positions in the public service, the employee must be able to carry out written instructions dependably and accurately. You may be given a chart with several columns, each column listing a variety of information. The questions require you to carry out directions involving the information given in the chart.

6) Skills and aptitudes

Performance tests effectively measure some manual skills and aptitudes. When the skill is one in which you are trained, such as typing or shorthand, you can practice. These tests are often very much like those given in business school or high school courses. For many of the other skills and aptitudes, however, no short-time preparation can be made. Skills and abilities natural to you or that you have developed throughout your lifetime are being tested.

Many of the general questions just described provide all the data needed to answer the questions and ask you to use your reasoning ability to find the answers. Your best preparation for these tests, as well as for tests of facts and ideas, is to be at your physical and mental best. You, no doubt, have your own methods of getting into an exam-taking mood and keeping "in shape." The next section lists some ideas on this subject.

IV. KINDS OF QUESTIONS

Only rarely is the "essay" question, which you answer in narrative form, used in civil service tests. Civil service tests are usually of the short-answer type. Full instructions for answering these questions will be given to you at the examination. But in case this is your first experience with short-answer questions and separate answer sheets, here is what you need to know:

1) Multiple-choice Questions

Most popular of the short-answer questions is the "multiple choice" or "best answer" question. It can be used, for example, to test for factual knowledge, ability to solve problems or judgment in meeting situations found at work.

A multiple-choice question is normally one of three types—
- It can begin with an incomplete statement followed by several possible endings. You are to find the one ending which *best* completes the statement, although some of the others may not be entirely wrong.
- It can also be a complete statement in the form of a question which is answered by choosing one of the statements listed.

- It can be in the form of a problem – again you select the best answer.

Here is an example of a multiple-choice question with a discussion which should give you some clues as to the method for choosing the right answer:

When an employee has a complaint about his assignment, the action which will *best* help him overcome his difficulty is to
    A. discuss his difficulty with his coworkers
    B. take the problem to the head of the organization
    C. take the problem to the person who gave him the assignment
    D. say nothing to anyone about his complaint

In answering this question, you should study each of the choices to find which is best. Consider choice "A" – Certainly an employee may discuss his complaint with fellow employees, but no change or improvement can result, and the complaint remains unresolved. Choice "B" is a poor choice since the head of the organization probably does not know what assignment you have been given, and taking your problem to him is known as "going over the head" of the supervisor. The supervisor, or person who made the assignment, is the person who can clarify it or correct any injustice. Choice "C" is, therefore, correct. To say nothing, as in choice "D," is unwise. Supervisors have and interest in knowing the problems employees are facing, and the employee is seeking a solution to his problem.

2) True/False Questions

The "true/false" or "right/wrong" form of question is sometimes used. Here a complete statement is given. Your job is to decide whether the statement is right or wrong.

SAMPLE: A roaming cell-phone call to a nearby city costs less than a non-roaming call to a distant city.

This statement is wrong, or false, since roaming calls are more expensive.

This is not a complete list of all possible question forms, although most of the others are variations of these common types. You will always get complete directions for answering questions. Be sure you understand *how* to mark your answers – ask questions until you do.

V. RECORDING YOUR ANSWERS

Computer terminals are used more and more today for many different kinds of exams.

For an examination with very few applicants, you may be told to record your answers in the test booklet itself. Separate answer sheets are much more common. If this separate answer sheet is to be scored by machine – and this is often the case – it is highly important that you mark your answers correctly in order to get credit.

An electronic scoring machine is often used in civil service offices because of the speed with which papers can be scored. Machine-scored answer sheets must be marked with a pencil, which will be given to you. This pencil has a high graphite content which responds to the electronic scoring machine. As a matter of fact, stray dots may register as answers, so do not let your pencil rest on the answer sheet while you are pondering the correct answer. Also, if your pencil lead breaks or is otherwise defective, ask for another.

Since the answer sheet will be dropped in a slot in the scoring machine, be careful not to bend the corners or get the paper crumpled.

The answer sheet normally has five vertical columns of numbers, with 30 numbers to a column. These numbers correspond to the question numbers in your test booklet. After each number, going across the page are four or five pairs of dotted lines. These short dotted lines have small letters or numbers above them. The first two pairs may also have a "T" or "F" above the letters. This indicates that the first two pairs only are to be used if the questions are of the true-false type. If the questions are multiple choice, disregard the "T" and "F" and pay attention only to the small letters or numbers.

Answer your questions in the manner of the sample that follows:

32. The largest city in the United States is
    A. Washington, D.C.
    B. New York City
    C. Chicago
    D. Detroit
    E. San Francisco

1) Choose the answer you think is best. (New York City is the largest, so "B" is correct.)
2) Find the row of dotted lines numbered the same as the question you are answering. (Find row number 32)
3) Find the pair of dotted lines corresponding to the answer. (Find the pair of lines under the mark "B.")
4) Make a solid black mark between the dotted lines.

VI. BEFORE THE TEST

Common sense will help you find procedures to follow to get ready for an examination. Too many of us, however, overlook these sensible measures. Indeed, nervousness and fatigue have been found to be the most serious reasons why applicants fail to do their best on civil service tests. Here is a list of reminders:

- Begin your preparation early – Don't wait until the last minute to go scurrying around for books and materials or to find out what the position is all about.
- Prepare continuously – An hour a night for a week is better than an all-night cram session. This has been definitely established. What is more, a night a week for a month will return better dividends than crowding your study into a shorter period of time.
- Locate the place of the exam – You have been sent a notice telling you when and where to report for the examination. If the location is in a different town or otherwise unfamiliar to you, it would be well to inquire the best route and learn something about the building.
- Relax the night before the test – Allow your mind to rest. Do not study at all that night. Plan some mild recreation or diversion; then go to bed early and get a good night's sleep.
- Get up early enough to make a leisurely trip to the place for the test – This way unforeseen events, traffic snarls, unfamiliar buildings, etc. will not upset you.
- Dress comfortably – A written test is not a fashion show. You will be known by number and not by name, so wear something comfortable.

- Leave excess paraphernalia at home – Shopping bags and odd bundles will get in your way. You need bring only the items mentioned in the official notice you received; usually everything you need is provided. Do not bring reference books to the exam. They will only confuse those last minutes and be taken away from you when in the test room.
- Arrive somewhat ahead of time – If because of transportation schedules you must get there very early, bring a newspaper or magazine to take your mind off yourself while waiting.
- Locate the examination room – When you have found the proper room, you will be directed to the seat or part of the room where you will sit. Sometimes you are given a sheet of instructions to read while you are waiting. Do not fill out any forms until you are told to do so; just read them and be prepared.
- Relax and prepare to listen to the instructions
- If you have any physical problem that may keep you from doing your best, be sure to tell the test administrator. If you are sick or in poor health, you really cannot do your best on the exam. You can come back and take the test some other time.

VII. AT THE TEST

The day of the test is here and you have the test booklet in your hand. The temptation to get going is very strong. Caution! There is more to success than knowing the right answers. You must know how to identify your papers and understand variations in the type of short-answer question used in this particular examination. Follow these suggestions for maximum results from your efforts:

1) Cooperate with the monitor

The test administrator has a duty to create a situation in which you can be as much at ease as possible. He will give instructions, tell you when to begin, check to see that you are marking your answer sheet correctly, and so on. He is not there to guard you, although he will see that your competitors do not take unfair advantage. He wants to help you do your best.

2) Listen to all instructions

Don't jump the gun! Wait until you understand all directions. In most civil service tests you get more time than you need to answer the questions. So don't be in a hurry. Read each word of instructions until you clearly understand the meaning. Study the examples, listen to all announcements and follow directions. Ask questions if you do not understand what to do.

3) Identify your papers

Civil service exams are usually identified by number only. You will be assigned a number; you must not put your name on your test papers. Be sure to copy your number correctly. Since more than one exam may be given, copy your exact examination title.

4) Plan your time

Unless you are told that a test is a "speed" or "rate of work" test, speed itself is usually not important. Time enough to answer all the questions will be provided, but this does not mean that you have all day. An overall time limit has been set. Divide the total time (in minutes) by the number of questions to determine the approximate time you have for each question.

5) Do not linger over difficult questions

If you come across a difficult question, mark it with a paper clip (useful to have along) and come back to it when you have been through the booklet. One caution if you do this – be sure to skip a number on your answer sheet as well. Check often to be sure that you have not lost your place and that you are marking in the row numbered the same as the question you are answering.

6) Read the questions

Be sure you know what the question asks! Many capable people are unsuccessful because they failed to *read* the questions correctly.

7) Answer all questions

Unless you have been instructed that a penalty will be deducted for incorrect answers, it is better to guess than to omit a question.

8) Speed tests

It is often better NOT to guess on speed tests. It has been found that on timed tests people are tempted to spend the last few seconds before time is called in marking answers at random – without even reading them – in the hope of picking up a few extra points. To discourage this practice, the instructions may warn you that your score will be "corrected" for guessing. That is, a penalty will be applied. The incorrect answers will be deducted from the correct ones, or some other penalty formula will be used.

9) Review your answers

If you finish before time is called, go back to the questions you guessed or omitted to give them further thought. Review other answers if you have time.

10) Return your test materials

If you are ready to leave before others have finished or time is called, take ALL your materials to the monitor and leave quietly. Never take any test material with you. The monitor can discover whose papers are not complete, and taking a test booklet may be grounds for disqualification.

VIII. EXAMINATION TECHNIQUES

1) Read the general instructions carefully. These are usually printed on the first page of the exam booklet. As a rule, these instructions refer to the timing of the examination; the fact that you should not start work until the signal and must stop work at a signal, etc. If there are any *special* instructions, such as a choice of questions to be answered, make sure that you note this instruction carefully.

2) When you are ready to start work on the examination, that is as soon as the signal has been given, read the instructions to each question booklet, underline any key words or phrases, such as *least, best, outline, describe* and the like. In this way you will tend to answer as requested rather than discover on reviewing your paper that you *listed without describing*, that you selected the *worst* choice rather than the *best* choice, etc.

3) If the examination is of the objective or multiple-choice type – that is, each question will also give a series of possible answers: A, B, C or D, and you are called upon to select the best answer and write the letter next to that answer on your answer paper – it is advisable to start answering each question in turn. There may be anywhere from 50 to 100 such questions in the three or four hours allotted and you can see how much time would be taken if you read through all the questions before beginning to answer any. Furthermore, if you come across a question or group of questions which you know would be difficult to answer, it would undoubtedly affect your handling of all the other questions.

4) If the examination is of the essay type and contains but a few questions, it is a moot point as to whether you should read all the questions before starting to answer any one. Of course, if you are given a choice – say five out of seven and the like – then it is essential to read all the questions so you can eliminate the two that are most difficult. If, however, you are asked to answer all the questions, there may be danger in trying to answer the easiest one first because you may find that you will spend too much time on it. The best technique is to answer the first question, then proceed to the second, etc.

5) Time your answers. Before the exam begins, write down the time it started, then add the time allowed for the examination and write down the time it must be completed, then divide the time available somewhat as follows:
    - If 3-1/2 hours are allowed, that would be 210 minutes. If you have 80 objective-type questions, that would be an average of 2-1/2 minutes per question. Allow yourself no more than 2 minutes per question, or a total of 160 minutes, which will permit about 50 minutes to review.
    - If for the time allotment of 210 minutes there are 7 essay questions to answer, that would average about 30 minutes a question. Give yourself only 25 minutes per question so that you have about 35 minutes to review.

6) The most important instruction is to *read each question* and make sure you know what is wanted. The second most important instruction is to *time yourself properly* so that you answer every question. The third most important instruction is to *answer every question*. Guess if you have to but include something for each question. Remember that you will receive no credit for a blank and will probably receive some credit if you write something in answer to an essay question. If you guess a letter – say "B" for a multiple-choice question – you may have guessed right. If you leave a blank as an answer to a multiple-choice question, the examiners may respect your feelings but it will not add a point to your score. Some exams may penalize you for wrong answers, so in such cases *only*, you may not want to guess unless you have some basis for your answer.

7) Suggestions
    a. Objective-type questions
        1. Examine the question booklet for proper sequence of pages and questions
        2. Read all instructions carefully
        3. Skip any question which seems too difficult; return to it after all other questions have been answered
        4. Apportion your time properly; do not spend too much time on any single question or group of questions

5. Note and underline key words – *all, most, fewest, least, best, worst, same, opposite,* etc.
6. Pay particular attention to negatives
7. Note unusual option, e.g., unduly long, short, complex, different or similar in content to the body of the question
8. Observe the use of "hedging" words – *probably, may, most likely,* etc.
9. Make sure that your answer is put next to the same number as the question
10. Do not second-guess unless you have good reason to believe the second answer is definitely more correct
11. Cross out original answer if you decide another answer is more accurate; do not erase until you are ready to hand your paper in
12. Answer all questions; guess unless instructed otherwise
13. Leave time for review

b. Essay questions
1. Read each question carefully
2. Determine exactly what is wanted. Underline key words or phrases.
3. Decide on outline or paragraph answer
4. Include many different points and elements unless asked to develop any one or two points or elements
5. Show impartiality by giving pros and cons unless directed to select one side only
6. Make and write down any assumptions you find necessary to answer the questions
7. Watch your English, grammar, punctuation and choice of words
8. Time your answers; don't crowd material

8) Answering the essay question

Most essay questions can be answered by framing the specific response around several key words or ideas. Here are a few such key words or ideas:

M's: manpower, materials, methods, money, management
P's: purpose, program, policy, plan, procedure, practice, problems, pitfalls, personnel, public relations

a. Six basic steps in handling problems:
1. Preliminary plan and background development
2. Collect information, data and facts
3. Analyze and interpret information, data and facts
4. Analyze and develop solutions as well as make recommendations
5. Prepare report and sell recommendations
6. Install recommendations and follow up effectiveness

b. Pitfalls to avoid
1. *Taking things for granted* – A statement of the situation does not necessarily imply that each of the elements is necessarily true; for example, a complaint may be invalid and biased so that all that can be taken for granted is that a complaint has been registered

2. *Considering only one side of a situation* – Wherever possible, indicate several alternatives and then point out the reasons you selected the best one
3. *Failing to indicate follow up* – Whenever your answer indicates action on your part, make certain that you will take proper follow-up action to see how successful your recommendations, procedures or actions turn out to be
4. *Taking too long in answering any single question* – Remember to time your answers properly

IX. AFTER THE TEST

Scoring procedures differ in detail among civil service jurisdictions although the general principles are the same. Whether the papers are hand-scored or graded by machine we have described, they are nearly always graded by number. That is, the person who marks the paper knows only the number – never the name – of the applicant. Not until all the papers have been graded will they be matched with names. If other tests, such as training and experience or oral interview ratings have been given, scores will be combined. Different parts of the examination usually have different weights. For example, the written test might count 60 percent of the final grade, and a rating of training and experience 40 percent. In many jurisdictions, veterans will have a certain number of points added to their grades.

After the final grade has been determined, the names are placed in grade order and an eligible list is established. There are various methods for resolving ties between those who get the same final grade – probably the most common is to place first the name of the person whose application was received first. Job offers are made from the eligible list in the order the names appear on it. You will be notified of your grade and your rank as soon as all these computations have been made. This will be done as rapidly as possible.

People who are found to meet the requirements in the announcement are called "eligibles." Their names are put on a list of eligible candidates. An eligible's chances of getting a job depend on how high he stands on this list and how fast agencies are filling jobs from the list.

When a job is to be filled from a list of eligibles, the agency asks for the names of people on the list of eligibles for that job. When the civil service commission receives this request, it sends to the agency the names of the three people highest on this list. Or, if the job to be filled has specialized requirements, the office sends the agency the names of the top three persons who meet these requirements from the general list.

The appointing officer makes a choice from among the three people whose names were sent to him. If the selected person accepts the appointment, the names of the others are put back on the list to be considered for future openings.

That is the rule in hiring from all kinds of eligible lists, whether they are for typist, carpenter, chemist, or something else. For every vacancy, the appointing officer has his choice of any one of the top three eligibles on the list. This explains why the person whose name is on top of the list sometimes does not get an appointment when some of the persons lower on the list do. If the appointing officer chooses the second or third eligible, the No. 1 eligible does not get a job at once, but stays on the list until he is appointed or the list is terminated.

X. HOW TO PASS THE INTERVIEW TEST

The examination for which you applied requires an oral interview test. You have already taken the written test and you are now being called for the interview test – the final part of the formal examination.

You may think that it is not possible to prepare for an interview test and that there are no procedures to follow during an interview. Our purpose is to point out some things you can do in advance that will help you and some good rules to follow and pitfalls to avoid while you are being interviewed.

What is an interview supposed to test?

The written examination is designed to test the technical knowledge and competence of the candidate; the oral is designed to evaluate intangible qualities, not readily measured otherwise, and to establish a list showing the relative fitness of each candidate – as measured against his competitors – for the position sought. Scoring is not on the basis of "right" and "wrong," but on a sliding scale of values ranging from "not passable" to "outstanding." As a matter of fact, it is possible to achieve a relatively low score without a single "incorrect" answer because of evident weakness in the qualities being measured.

Occasionally, an examination may consist entirely of an oral test – either an individual or a group oral. In such cases, information is sought concerning the technical knowledges and abilities of the candidate, since there has been no written examination for this purpose. More commonly, however, an oral test is used to supplement a written examination.

Who conducts interviews?

The composition of oral boards varies among different jurisdictions. In nearly all, a representative of the personnel department serves as chairman. One of the members of the board may be a representative of the department in which the candidate would work. In some cases, "outside experts" are used, and, frequently, a businessman or some other representative of the general public is asked to serve. Labor and management or other special groups may be represented. The aim is to secure the services of experts in the appropriate field.

However the board is composed, it is a good idea (and not at all improper or unethical) to ascertain in advance of the interview who the members are and what groups they represent. When you are introduced to them, you will have some idea of their backgrounds and interests, and at least you will not stutter and stammer over their names.

What should be done before the interview?

While knowledge about the board members is useful and takes some of the surprise element out of the interview, there is other preparation which is more substantive. It *is* possible to prepare for an oral interview – in several ways:

1) Keep a copy of your application and review it carefully before the interview

This may be the only document before the oral board, and the starting point of the interview. Know what education and experience you have listed there, and the sequence and dates of all of it. Sometimes the board will ask you to review the highlights of your experience for them; you should not have to hem and haw doing it.

2) Study the class specification and the examination announcement

Usually, the oral board has one or both of these to guide them. The qualities, characteristics or knowledges required by the position sought are stated in these documents. They offer valuable clues as to the nature of the oral interview. For example, if the job involves supervisory responsibilities, the announcement will usually indicate that knowledge of modern supervisory methods and the qualifications of the candidate as a supervisor will be tested. If so, you can expect such questions, frequently in the form of a hypothetical situation which you are expected to solve. NEVER go into an oral without knowledge of the duties and responsibilities of the job you seek.

3) Think through each qualification required

Try to visualize the kind of questions you would ask if you were a board member. How well could you answer them? Try especially to appraise your own knowledge and background in each area, *measured against the job sought*, and identify any areas in which you are weak. Be critical and realistic – do not flatter yourself.

4) Do some general reading in areas in which you feel you may be weak

For example, if the job involves supervision and your past experience has NOT, some general reading in supervisory methods and practices, particularly in the field of human relations, might be useful. Do NOT study agency procedures or detailed manuals. The oral board will be testing your understanding and capacity, not your memory.

5) Get a good night's sleep and watch your general health and mental attitude

You will want a clear head at the interview. Take care of a cold or any other minor ailment, and of course, no hangovers.

What should be done on the day of the interview?

Now comes the day of the interview itself. Give yourself plenty of time to get there. Plan to arrive somewhat ahead of the scheduled time, particularly if your appointment is in the fore part of the day. If a previous candidate fails to appear, the board might be ready for you a bit early. By early afternoon an oral board is almost invariably behind schedule if there are many candidates, and you may have to wait. Take along a book or magazine to read, or your application to review, but leave any extraneous material in the waiting room when you go in for your interview. In any event, relax and compose yourself.

The matter of dress is important. The board is forming impressions about you – from your experience, your manners, your attitude, and your appearance. Give your personal appearance careful attention. Dress your best, but not your flashiest. Choose conservative, appropriate clothing, and be sure it is immaculate. This is a business interview, and your appearance should indicate that you regard it as such. Besides, being well groomed and properly dressed will help boost your confidence.

Sooner or later, someone will call your name and escort you into the interview room. *This is it.* From here on you are on your own. It is too late for any more preparation. But remember, you asked for this opportunity to prove your fitness, and you are here because your request was granted.

What happens when you go in?

The usual sequence of events will be as follows: The clerk (who is often the board stenographer) will introduce you to the chairman of the oral board, who will introduce you to the other members of the board. Acknowledge the introductions before you sit down. Do not be surprised if you find a microphone facing you or a stenotypist sitting by. Oral interviews are usually recorded in the event of an appeal or other review.

Usually the chairman of the board will open the interview by reviewing the highlights of your education and work experience from your application – primarily for the benefit of the other members of the board, as well as to get the material into the record. Do not interrupt or comment unless there is an error or significant misinterpretation; if that is the case, do not hesitate. But do not quibble about insignificant matters. Also, he will usually ask you some question about your education, experience or your present job – partly to get you to start talking and to establish the interviewing "rapport." He may start the actual questioning, or turn it over to one of the other members. Frequently, each member undertakes the questioning on a particular area, one in which he is perhaps most competent, so you can expect each member to participate in the examination. Because time is limited, you may also expect some rather abrupt switches in the direction the questioning takes, so do not be upset by it. Normally, a board member will not pursue a single line of questioning unless he discovers a particular strength or weakness.

After each member has participated, the chairman will usually ask whether any member has any further questions, then will ask you if you have anything you wish to add. Unless you are expecting this question, it may floor you. Worse, it may start you off on an extended, extemporaneous speech. The board is not usually seeking more information. The question is principally to offer you a last opportunity to present further qualifications or to indicate that you have nothing to add. So, if you feel that a significant qualification or characteristic has been overlooked, it is proper to point it out in a sentence or so. Do not compliment the board on the thoroughness of their examination – they have been sketchy, and you know it. If you wish, merely say, "No thank you, I have nothing further to add." This is a point where you can "talk yourself out" of a good impression or fail to present an important bit of information. Remember, *you close the interview yourself.*

The chairman will then say, "That is all, Mr. _____, thank you." Do not be startled; the interview is over, and quicker than you think. Thank him, gather your belongings and take your leave. Save your sigh of relief for the other side of the door.

How to put your best foot forward
Throughout this entire process, you may feel that the board individually and collectively is trying to pierce your defenses, seek out your hidden weaknesses and embarrass and confuse you. Actually, this is not true. They are obliged to make an appraisal of your qualifications for the job you are seeking, and they want to see you in your best light. Remember, they must interview all candidates and a non-cooperative candidate may become a failure in spite of their best efforts to bring out his qualifications. Here are 15 suggestions that will help you:

1) Be natural – Keep your attitude confident, not cocky
If you are not confident that you can do the job, do not expect the board to be. Do not apologize for your weaknesses, try to bring out your strong points. The board is interested in a positive, not negative, presentation. Cockiness will antagonize any board member and make him wonder if you are covering up a weakness by a false show of strength.

2) Get comfortable, but don't lounge or sprawl
Sit erectly but not stiffly. A careless posture may lead the board to conclude that you are careless in other things, or at least that you are not impressed by the importance of the occasion. Either conclusion is natural, even if incorrect. Do not fuss with your clothing, a pencil or an ashtray. Your hands may occasionally be useful to emphasize a point; do not let them become a point of distraction.

3) Do not wisecrack or make small talk
This is a serious situation, and your attitude should show that you consider it as such. Further, the time of the board is limited – they do not want to waste it, and neither should you.

4) Do not exaggerate your experience or abilities
In the first place, from information in the application or other interviews and sources, the board may know more about you than you think. Secondly, you probably will not get away with it. An experienced board is rather adept at spotting such a situation, so do not take the chance.

5) If you know a board member, do not make a point of it, yet do not hide it
Certainly you are not fooling him, and probably not the other members of the board. Do not try to take advantage of your acquaintanceship – it will probably do you little good.

6) Do not dominate the interview
Let the board do that. They will give you the clues – do not assume that you have to do all the talking. Realize that the board has a number of questions to ask you, and do not try to take up all the interview time by showing off your extensive knowledge of the answer to the first one.

7) Be attentive
You only have 20 minutes or so, and you should keep your attention at its sharpest throughout. When a member is addressing a problem or question to you, give him your undivided attention. Address your reply principally to him, but do not exclude the other board members.

8) Do not interrupt
A board member may be stating a problem for you to analyze. He will ask you a question when the time comes. Let him state the problem, and wait for the question.

9) Make sure you understand the question
Do not try to answer until you are sure what the question is. If it is not clear, restate it in your own words or ask the board member to clarify it for you. However, do not haggle about minor elements.

10) Reply promptly but not hastily
A common entry on oral board rating sheets is "candidate responded readily," or "candidate hesitated in replies." Respond as promptly and quickly as you can, but do not jump to a hasty, ill-considered answer.

11) Do not be peremptory in your answers
A brief answer is proper – but do not fire your answer back. That is a losing game from your point of view. The board member can probably ask questions much faster than you can answer them.

12) Do not try to create the answer you think the board member wants
He is interested in what kind of mind you have and how it works – not in playing games. Furthermore, he can usually spot this practice and will actually grade you down on it.

13) Do not switch sides in your reply merely to agree with a board member
Frequently, a member will take a contrary position merely to draw you out and to see if you are willing and able to defend your point of view. Do not start a debate, yet do not surrender a good position. If a position is worth taking, it is worth defending.

14) Do not be afraid to admit an error in judgment if you are shown to be wrong

The board knows that you are forced to reply without any opportunity for careful consideration. Your answer may be demonstrably wrong. If so, admit it and get on with the interview.

15) Do not dwell at length on your present job

The opening question may relate to your present assignment. Answer the question but do not go into an extended discussion. You are being examined for a *new* job, not your present one. As a matter of fact, try to phrase ALL your answers in terms of the job for which you are being examined.

Basis of Rating

Probably you will forget most of these "do's" and "don'ts" when you walk into the oral interview room. Even remembering them all will not ensure you a passing grade. Perhaps you did not have the qualifications in the first place. But remembering them will help you to put your best foot forward, without treading on the toes of the board members.

Rumor and popular opinion to the contrary notwithstanding, an oral board wants you to make the best appearance possible. They know you are under pressure – but they also want to see how you respond to it as a guide to what your reaction would be under the pressures of the job you seek. They will be influenced by the degree of poise you display, the personal traits you show and the manner in which you respond.

ABOUT THIS BOOK

This book contains tests divided into Examination Sections. Go through each test, answering every question in the margin. We have also attached a sample answer sheet at the back of the book that can be removed and used. At the end of each test look at the answer key and check your answers. On the ones you got wrong, look at the right answer choice and learn. Do not fill in the answers first. Do not memorize the questions and answers, but understand the answer and principles involved. On your test, the questions will likely be different from the samples. Questions are changed and new ones added. If you understand these past questions you should have success with any changes that arise. Tests may consist of several types of questions. We have additional books on each subject should more study be advisable or necessary for you. Finally, the more you study, the better prepared you will be. This book is intended to be the last thing you study before you walk into the examination room. Prior study of relevant texts is also recommended. NLC publishes some of these in our Fundamental Series. Knowledge and good sense are important factors in passing your exam. Good luck also helps. So now study this Passbook, absorb the material contained within and take that knowledge into the examination. Then do your best to pass that exam.

EXAMINATION SECTION

EXAMINATION SECTION
TEST 1

DIRECTIONS: Each question or incomplete statement is followed by several suggested answers or completions. Select the one that BEST answers the question or completes the statement. *PRINT THE LETTER OF THE CORRECT ANSWER IN THE SPACE AT THE RIGHT.*

1. The three main types of computer programming languages are
   A. C++, Fortran, COBOL
   B. high level language, assembly language, and machine language
   C. declarative language, functional language, and imperative language
   D. none of the above

   1.____

2. The purpose of using subroutines in larger programs is NOT
   A. the reduction of storage equipment
   B. the increment in programming ease
   C. for making program testing easy at the time of development
   D. the reduction of execution time of program

   2.____

3. Variables accessible in inner block are those declared in the _____ block.
   A. outer
   B. same
   C. inner
   D. all of the above

   3.____

4. Execution order of recursive function is
   A. parallel
   B. last in first out
   C. first in first out
   D. none of the above

   4.____

5. Which of the following is NOT true about dynamic type checking?
   A. It provides more flexibility to the programmer
   B. It slows down the execution
   C. Both A and B
   D. None of the above

   5.____

6. Assume that z >=0, w = 0, do while (w < z), w = 2 + 7, loop.
   After the execution of the above code, which of the following statements will be true?
   A. w may be equal to x
   B. w may be equal to x + 7
   C. w must be greater than 0
   D. w must be greater than z

   6.____

7. If a function returns _____, then the type of function must be declared in the calling program.
   A. non-integer value
   B. integer value
   C. both A and B
   D. neither A nor B

   7.____

1

8. A function that _____ is an inline function.
   A. does not return anything
   B. uses function definition instead of function call
   C. is self-calling
   D. none of the above

9. get value
   while value is negative
   add to sum of previous values
   The above given pseudo code is an example of a(n)
   A. nested loop   B. loop
   C. decision   D. sequence

10. Which is the condition for which sequence logic cannot be used?
    A. When two numbers are added
    B. When two data sets are compared
    C. When the output is given to user
    D. When the input is accepted from user

11. _____ is a prototype that defines those variables and methods which are common to all objects of some particular type.
    A. Polymorphism   B. Inheritance
    C. Class   D. Aggregation

12. Which of the following OOP concepts define the relationship between super class and subclass?
    A. Polymorphism   B. Encapsulation
    C. Inheritance   D. Scalability

13. In object-oriented programming, redundancy is reduced by
    A. code re-usage
    B. integration of different systems
    C. reduction in size of developed system
    D. reducing lines of code

Questions 14-16.

DIRECTIONS: Questions 14 through 16 are to be answered on the basis of the following figure.

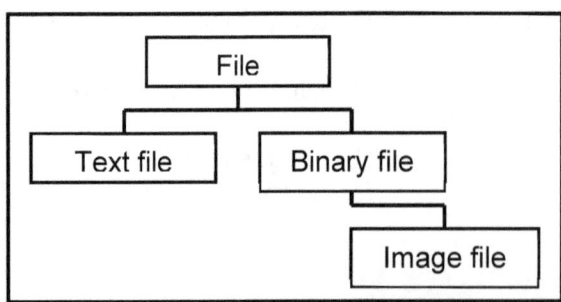

14. Which of the following statements is INCORRECT?
    A. Super class file has two subclasses: Text file and Binary file.
    B. Image file is a Binary file and file.
    C. Text file is Binary file and file.
    D. Array of files may hold Binary file and Text file.

15. Which of the following is CORRECT assuming that file and Binary file are abstract classes and Text file and Image file are concrete classes?
    A. File object can be instantiated only if it is assigned to Binary file reference.
    B. Image file object can be instantiated and assigned to either file reference or Binary file reference.
    C. Image file object can be instantiated and assigned to Text file reference.
    D. Binary file object can be instantiated and assigned to file reference.

16. Assuming file as an abstract class and Image file and Binary file as concrete classes, a method name toFile is implemented in both Image file and Binary file. A file object references an Image file object in memory and calls toFile method, implementation method of which class will be called
    A. Binary file   B. Image file
    C. Text file   D. none of the above

17. Objective of program, required inputs, target outputs, and all requirements for processing are kept in the
    A. specification document of program
    B. project management database
    C. tracking log of program
    D. management information system

18. Who prepares the technical documentation of a program?
    A. Manager   B. User
    C. Marketing person   D. Coder

19. Graphical representation of detailed steps that are needed to solve a problem is called
    A. desk checking   B. syntax
    C. flowchart   D. pseudo code

20. In a flowchart, the symbol shown at the right represents
    A. decision
    B. output
    C. input
    D. termination

Questions 21-22.

DIRECTIONS: Questions 21 and 22 are to be answered on the basis of the following flowchart.

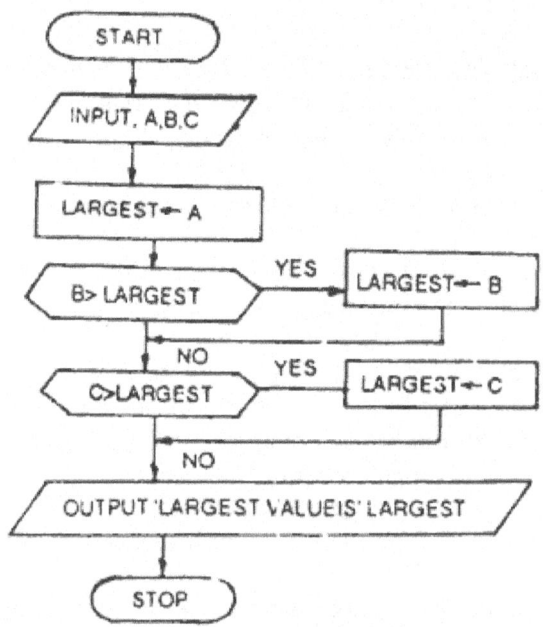

21. Which of the following problems is this flowchart representing?
    A. Finding largest of A, B, and C
    B. Finding average value of A, B, and C
    C. Finding lowest of A, B, and C
    D. Comparing A, B, and C

21._____

22. The output of this program will be
    A. largest number
    B. average number
    C. least number
    D. stop

22._____

23. Which of the following sketch out all the details of the program?
    A. Algorithm
    B. Flowchart
    C. Macro flowchart
    D. Micro flowchart

23._____

24. Document flowchart is useful for
    A. analysis of system
    B. analyzing the capability of control procedures
    C. identification of inputs
    D. none of the above

24._____

25. In a data flow diagram, which of the following symbols represents data flow?
    A. Parallel lines   B. Circle   C. Arrow   D. Square

25._____

KEY (CORRECT ANSWERS)

1. B
2. C
3. D
4. B
5. C

6. D
7. A
8. B
9. B
10. B

11. C
12. C
13. A
14. B
15. B

16. B
17. A
18. D
19. C
20. A

21. A
22. A
23. D
24. B
25. C

TEST 2

DIRECTIONS: Each question or incomplete statement is followed by several suggested answers or completions. Select the one that BEST answers the question or completes the statement. *PRINT THE LETTER OF THE CORRECT ANSWER IN THE SPACE AT THE RIGHT.*

1. From a programmer's viewpoint, the main advantage of using a high-level programming language rather than a machine or assembly language is
   A. efficiency
   B. ease of development
   C. portability of program
   D. none of the above

   1.____

2. Scope of local variable is
   A. global
   B. local
   C. only within the current program
   D. outside the current program

   2.____

3. Type of value that a variable can store is identified by
   A. name of variable
   B. data type
   C. size of variable
   D. none of the above

   3.____

4. A chunk of statements that executes a coherent task of some type is called
   A. program body
   B. loop
   C. function
   D. statement

   4.____

5. The following is a recursive function f(z), if (z > 100), return (z – 10), else return (f(f(z + 11))).
   What value of z gives f(z) = 91?
   A. 1
   B. 91
   C. 101
   D. All of the above

   5.____

6. Which of the following is TRUE about aliasing?
   A. More than one name can be associated with any particular location.
   B. Two commands have the same code but different names.
   C. Both A and B
   D. None of the above

   6.____

7. In which situation does parameter passing give different results for call by name and call by reference?
   When _____ is passed as a parameter.
   A. an array element
   B. pointer
   C. an array
   D. an expression

   7.____

8. For structured programming, which of the following principles should NOT be followed?
   A. Good programming approach should be used.
   B. Program should be coded in a way that it is executed flawlessly without testing.
   C. Program should be designed using top down approach.
   D. Each module of program should be written as control structure series.

   8.____

9. get value
   get another value
   if second value is bigger than first value
   print second value
   else
   print first value
   The above given pseudo code is an example of a(n)
   A. nested loop   B. loop   C. decision   D. sequence

10. Infinite loops can be avoided by using
    A. for   B. do while   C. while   D. sentinel

11. In object oriented programming, communication of objects of different classes is done by
    A. messages
    B. inheritance
    C. concealment
    D. polymorphism

12. Using method overriding, which of the following is CORRECT? The overridden method can be determined by
    A. method signature
    B. class
    C. object reference
    D. number of parameters

13. An aggregate object is an object instance
    A. containing other objects
    B. with primitive attributes only
    C. with static methods only
    D. with instances methods and primitive attributes

14. Which of the following is NOT true about objects?
    A. Objects do not allow encapsulation.
    B. Both static and instance data can be accessed by objects.
    C. Object class is extended by all classes.
    D. None of the above

15. Which of the following is TRUE about private instance variable?
    A. Method defined outside the class can modify it.
    B. Method defined outside the class can modify it only if it is returned by method
    C. Method defined outside the class can modify it only if it is returned by method and if it is of the same class type
    D. None of the above

16. Which of the following statements is CORRECT about protected derivation from base class to derived class?
    A. Derived class' protected members are those which were base class' private members.
    B. Derived class' protected members are those which were base class' public members.
    C. Derived class' public members are those which were base class' protected members.
    D. None of the above

17. While generating specification of a program, end user must clear out the desired
    A. icon   B. splash logo   C. output   D. input

18. It is important to document computer programs so that
    A. program can be learned by user
    B. programmers can locate sources of errors easily
    C. program maintenance will be easy for other developers
    D. all of the above

19. In a flowchart, the symbol shown at the right represents
    A. decision
    B. output
    C. input
    D. termination

Questions 20-23.

DIRECTIONS: Questions 20 through 23 are to be answered on the basis of the following figure.

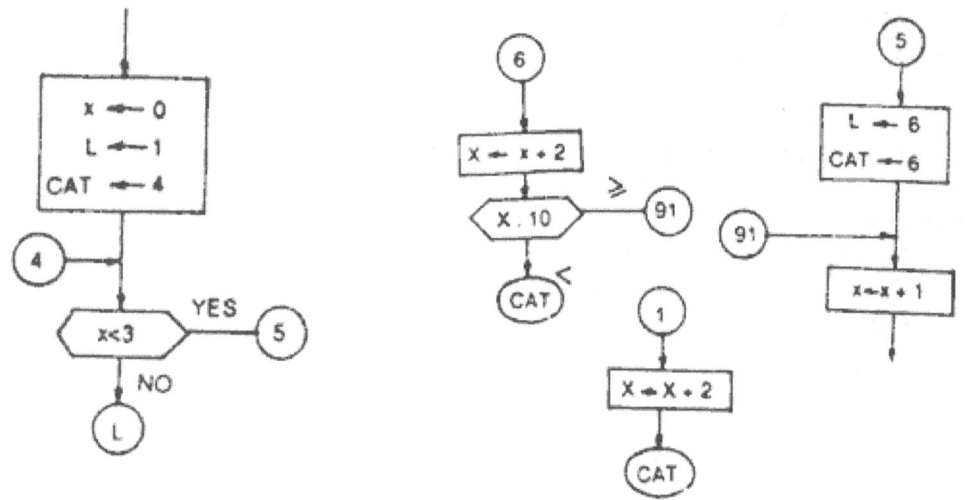

20. Which of the following are label constants in the given flowchart? 20.____
    A. 91, 6, 5, 1, 4
    B. 4, 6, 5, 1
    C. 5 and 4 only
    D. 4 and 1 only

21. Which of the following are variables? 21.____
    A. X, 91, CAT, and L
    B. 91, CAT and L
    C. CAT and L
    D. None of the above

22. Which of the following are in-connectors? 22.____
    A. 6, 5, 91, 4, 1
    B. 5, 4, 91, 1
    C. 1, 4, 91
    D. 91, 4

23. Which of the following are out-connectors? 23.____
    A. L, 5
    B. 5, 91
    C. 1, 91
    D. 91, L, 5, CAT

24. That chart that shows only flow of function but no code is known as 24.____
    A. structure chart
    B. flowchart
    C. both A and B
    D. none of the above

25. While drawing DFD, which of the following is not required? 25.____
    A. Development of systems flowchart
    B. Determination of system boundaries
    C. Subdividing the DFD
    D. Developing a context diagram

KEY (CORRECT ANSWERS)

1.	B		11.	A
2.	C		12.	B
3.	B		13.	A
4.	C		14.	A
5.	D		15.	C
6.	C		16.	B
7.	D		17.	C
8.	C		18.	D
9.	C		19.	D
10.	D		20.	A

21. C
22. A
23. D
24. A
25. A

TEST 3

DIRECTIONS: Each question or incomplete statement is followed by several suggested answers or completions. Select the one that BEST answers the question or completes the statement. *PRINT THE LETTER OF THE CORRECT ANSWER IN THE SPACE AT THE RIGHT.*

1. The limitations of high level programming languages is(are) 1.____
   A. large execution time
   B. less optimization of code
   C. management of increasing complexity
   D. all of the above

2. The local variable can be accessed from 2.____
   A. the block where it is declared
   B. main
   C. function
   D. both A and C

3. The scope of the globally declared variable is 3.____
   A. throughout the whole program
   B. restricted to the function where it is declared
   C. inside the outer block
   D. none of the above

4. A variable has to be passed as an actual argument. This statement is correct for which parameter passing mechanism: 4.____
   I. Pass by reference
   II. Pass by result of value
   III. Pass by result
   IV. Pass by value

   The CORRECT answer is:
   A. II and III only
   B. I and IV only
   C. I, II, and III
   D. None of the above

5. Which of the following statements is CORRECT? 5.____
   A. Iteration and recursion are evenly powerful.
   B. Recursive function has always an equivalent iterative function.
   C. Unlike recursion, iteration completely executes the body each time the termination condition is set.
   D. All of the above

6. An array is passed by _____ when it is used as a function argument. 6.____
   A. name
   B. reference
   C. value
   D. none of the above

7.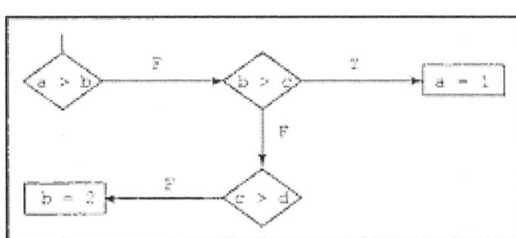

Which of the following lines of code implements the above flowchart correctly?

I. If (a>b)
    ;
    else if (b>c)
    a = 1
    else if (c>d)
    ;
    else b = 2

II. if (a>b)
    ;
    else if (b>c)
    a = 1;
    else if (c<=d)
    b = 2;

III. if (a<=b)
    if (b>c)
    a = 1;
    else if (c<=)
    b = 2;

IV. if (a>b)
    if (b>c)
    a = 1;
    else if (c>d)
    b = 2;

The CORRECT answer is:
A. I and IV only
B. III and IV only
C. I, II, and III
D. None of the above

8. Prototype declaration is necessary when
   A. a function is called before its definition
   B. any function is called
   C. a function is defined before it is called
   D. all of the above

9. get value
    get another value
    add values
    print resultant values
    The above given pseudo code is an example of a(n)
    A. nested loop
    B. loop
    C. decision
    D. sequence

10. The while loop is an entry controlled loop.
    A. False
    B. True
    C. Condition dependent
    D. None of the above

11. If an object has many forms, then which of the following OOP concepts logically holds true?
    A. Polymorphism
    B. Encapsulation
    C. Inheritance
    D. Scalability

12. A collection of declared constants and method is called _____. When a(n) _____ is implemented by a class, it ensures that all the declared methods in that _____ will be implemented.
    A. object
    B. interface
    C. class
    D. exception

13. Which method can access the private attribute? 13.____
    A. Classes of the same package
    B. Static methods of the same class
    C. Instance methods of the same class
    D. Methods defined in the same class

14. Which of the following can achieve runtime polymorphism? 14.____
    A. Overloading of operator   B. Friend function
    C. Overloading of function   D. Virtual function

15. A pure virtual function is the one which 15.____
    A. is called to delete an object
    B. consists of full function body
    C. has its definition only in derived class
    D. none of the above

16. Which of the following should be carried out during all the programming steps? 16.____
    A. Beta testing   B. Design
    C. Coding   D. Documentation

17. User documentation may contain instructions 17.____
    A. to prepare input of a program
    B. about to whom output must be distributed
    C. about how often program needs to run
    D. all of the above

18. _____ are an essential part of program documentation. 18.____
    A. Symbols   B. Comments
    C. Both of the above   D. None of the above

19. In a flowchart, the symbol shown at the right represents 19.____
    A. input/output
    B. decision
    C. process
    D. terminator

Questions 20-24.

DIRECTIONS: Questions 20 through 24 are to be answered on the basis of the following figure.

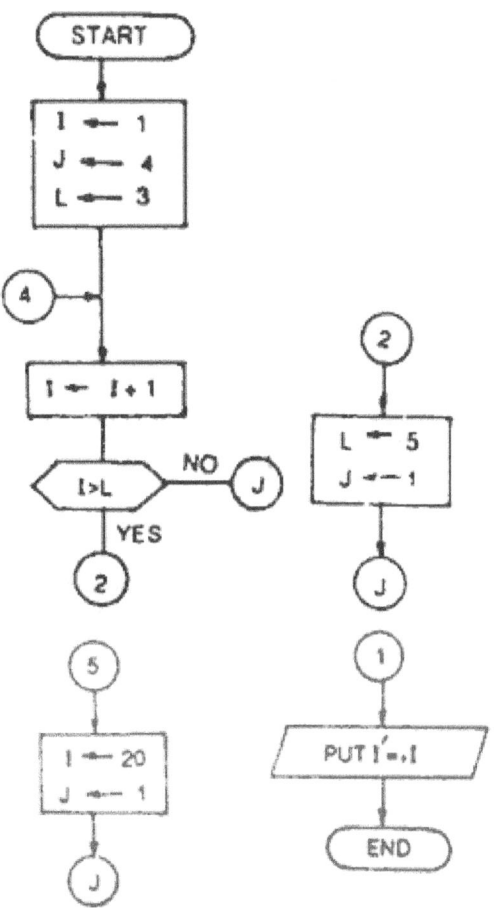

20. Which of the following are label constants?
    A. 6, 5, 2, 4, 1   B. 4, 5, 2, 1   C. 2, 4, 1   D. 1

21. Which of the following are liable variables?
    A. I, J
    B. I
    C. J
    D. None of the above

22. Symbol I is executed _____ number of times.
    A. 2   B. 3   C. 4   D. 1

23. When symbol 2 is executed, what is the value of I?
    A. 8   B. 6   C. 4   D. 2

24. Which of the following are numeric constants?
    A. 20, 5, 1, 3
    B. 5, 1, 3
    C. 3, 1
    D. None of the above

25. While constructing a flowchart, which of the following guidelines should be followed? 25.____
    A. Make assumption that a reader may know the flow direction
    B. Normal flow of operation should be flowcharted only
    C. Identification of entities that should be flowcharted
    D. Both B and C

KEY (CORRECT ANSWERS)

1.	D		11.	A
2.	D		12.	B
3.	A		13.	D
4.	C		14.	D
5.	D		15.	C
6.	B		16.	D
7.	C		17.	D
8.	A		18.	B
9.	D		19.	C
10.	B		20.	B

21.	C
22.	B
23.	C
24.	A
25.	D

TEST 4

DIRECTIONS: Each question or incomplete statement is followed by several suggested answers or completions. Select the one that BEST answers the question or completes the statement. *PRINT THE LETTER OF THE CORRECT ANSWER IN THE SPACE AT THE RIGHT.*

1. For the same problem, one piece of code has 100 instructions and another piece of code has 200 instructions. Which of the following statements is logically CORRECT?
   A. Execution time of both sets of instructions is the same
   B. Execution time of the first is less than the second
   C. Compilation time of the first is less than the second
   D. None of the above

   1.____

2. Which of the following tells the difference between applicative and procedural languages:
   I. Applicative predominantly evaluates the expressions.
   II. Applicative uses parameters to communicate value instead of assignment statement
   III. Procedural predominantly evaluates the expressions
   IV. Procedural uses parameters to communicate value instead of assignment statement

   The CORRECT answer is:
   A. I and II only
   B. III and IV only
   C. II and III only
   D. None of the above

   2.____

3. Priority order for local and global variable is
   A. first global then local
   B. first local then global
   C. same priority order for both
   D. none of the above

   3.____

4. A program module may not have which of the following characteristics?
   A. Self-contained
   B. Size is relatively small
   C. Includes many sub modules
   D. Performs a particular job

   4.____

5. The advantages of using recursion are
   I. Improvement in logical clarity
   II. Ease in debugging process
   III. Reduction in execution time
   IV. Reduction in code size

   The CORRECT answer is:
   A. I and II only
   B. I, II, and III
   C. I and IV only
   D. None of the above

   5.____

6. Replacing the function by its value without making any changes in the meaning. This phenomena is known as
   A. unbinding
   B. dynamic binding
   C. referential transparence
   D. none of the above

   6.____

7. Assume that z >= 0
   w = 1
   do while (w<=z)
     w=w*2
   Loop
   After the above code is executed, which of the following given statements will be INCORRECT?
   A. w must be a power of 2
   B. w may be equal to z+1
   C. w may be equal to z
   D. w may be odd

8. Pointers to _____ are the same as array of pointers.
   A. structures   B. functions   C. pointers   D. array

9. Which of the following is an advantage of inline function?
   A. Smaller program size
   B. Faster execution
   C. Both A and B
   D. None of the above

10. If a program repeats a chunk of code until it meets a certain condition, it is an example of _____ structure.
    A. do while
    B. do until
    C. what if
    D. if then else

11. Which of the following OOP concepts illustrates the object's internal representation that cannot be viewed outside the definition of object?
    A. Polymorphism
    B. Encapsulation
    C. Inheritance
    D. Expandable

12. A class having the same number of methods but different number of parameters is called method
    A. overriding   B. invocating   C. overloading   D. labeling

13. Which of the following can BEST define polymorphism?
    A. A technique that is used by objects to call up different methods depending upon the type of control structure
    B. A technique that is used by objects to call up overridden methods depending upon the type of application
    C. A technique in which any object produced from the class can be referred to by object reference
    D. None of the above

14. The void return type means
    A. Not a valid return type
    B. It returns no data type
    C. It returns void area in memory
    D. None of the above

15. Pointer to base class stores the address of
    A. object of derived class only
    B. object of base class only
    C. objects of base class and derived class as well
    D. none of the above

16. Which statements are true about the difference of constructor and destructor?
    I.   Constructor takes arguments but destructor does not.
    II. It is possible for constructor to be overloaded but destructor does not overload.
    III. Destructor takes arguments but constructor does not.
    IV. It is possible for destructor to be overloaded but constructor does not overload.

    The CORRECT answer is:
    A. I and II only
    B. III and IV only
    C. II and III only
    D. None of the above

17. Standards used in documentation are
    A. comments
    B. Hungarian notations
    C. description of functions
    D. all of the above

18. Tools for documentation are important because
    A. internal control system can be evaluated through them
    B. system flow can be determined by using them
    C. both of the above
    D. none of the above

19. Pseudo code and flowcharts are tools that are used in the program _____ phase.
    A. code
    B. design
    C. test
    D. specification

20. In a flowchart, the symbol shown at the right represents
    A. in connector
    B. input/output
    C. annotation
    D. termination

21. Which of the following sketch out the main part of the program?
    A. Algorithm
    B. Flowchart
    C. Macro flowchart
    D. Micro flowchart

22. A tool that contains all the symbols needed to draw the flowchart is called
    A. operations
    B. template
    C. note
    D. none of the above

23. The number of flow lines leaving the decision symbol are
    A. more than 2
    B. 1 or 2
    C. 2 only
    D. 1 only

24. A graphical tool that describes the flow of data in the system, source and destinations of data as well as the processes that store and transform the data is called
    A. flowchart of system
    B. flowchart of program
    C. document flowchart
    D. data flow diagram

25. In data flow diagrams, circles represent
    A. data stores
    B. transformation processes
    C. flow of data
    D. source and destination of data

KEY (CORRECT ANSWERS)

1.	D		11.	B
2.	A		12.	C
3.	B		13.	C
4.	B		14.	B
5.	C		15.	C
6.	C		16.	A
7.	C		17.	D
8.	C		18.	C
9.	B		19.	B
10.	B		20.	B

21. C
22. B
23. C
24. D
25. B

EXAMINATION SECTION
TEST 1

DIRECTIONS: Each question or incomplete statement is followed by several suggested answers or completions. Select the one that BEST answers the question or completes the statement. *PRINT THE LETTER OF THE CORRECT ANSWER IN THE SPACE AT THE RIGHT.*

1. The time complexity of merger sort algorithm is
   A. O(n)   B. O(n log n)   C. O(log n)   D. O(n2)

2. Polymorphism refers to the
   A. process of returning data from a function referencing
   B. specialization of classes through inheritance
   C. uses of classes to represent objects
   D. packaging of data defining an object as private

3. A stack has two primary operations:
   A. push and pull   B. push and pop
   C. insert and delete   D. append and delete

4. Efficiency of an algorithm is measured as
   A. time and space   B. runtime and space
   C. complexity and capacity D. processor and memory

5. If class D inherits from class B, suppose a function f() is defined for the base class. In what ways can D make use of ()?
   A. It can inherit, extend or reject f()
   B. It can make f() abstract, virtual or overloaded
   C. It can replace, extend or inherit f()
   D. It can overload, replace or reject f()

6. The correct syntax for calling a base class constructor in the definition of derived class of derived class constructor is
   A. derived class::derived class () {base class ();}
   B. derived class::base class () {derived class,}
   C. derived class::derived class () : base class () {}
   D. derived class::base class () : derived class () { }

7. Which function is used to move the file pointer for the output in C++?
   A. Stream.seekg(length);   B. Stream.seekp(length);
   C. Stream.tellg();   D. None of the above

8. The complier performs _____ on virtual functions.
   A. static binding   B. dynamic binding
   C. additional error checking D. none of the above

9. In which phase of system development process the technical blueprint and specifications for a solution to fulfill the business requirements are developed?
   A. System initiation
   B. System implementation
   C. System design
   D. Feasibility study

10. System requirements are created during
    A. preliminary investigation
    B. analysis
    C. design
    D. development

11. The activity-based model in which each phase is performed sequentially from planning through implementation and maintenance is called
    A. waterfall model
    B. spiral model
    C. raid model
    D. none of the above

12. When is the derived class constructor called relative to the base class constructor?
    A. They are called together
    B. Depends on kind of derivation
    C. Derived class constructor first
    D. Base class constructor first

13. Consider the following tree with the root node labeled as L:

    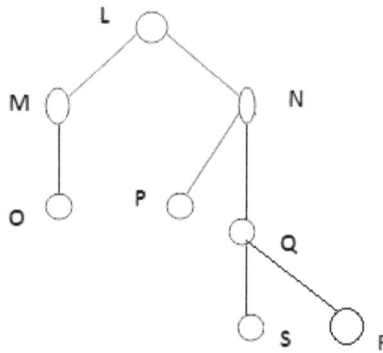

    The in-order traversals for these nodes are
    A. OMLPNSQR   B. OMLPQNSR   C. OMLPSQRN   D. OMLPNQSR

14. If the int variable i, j and k contains the values 3, 20, 100, respectively, what is the value of the following logical expression:
    j<4 || j == 5 && i < 3 && k<4 || 20 ==5 && 3<100

    A. True   B. False   C. None

15. After execution of the following code, what will be the value of the angle if the input value of the angle is 0?
    ```
    If (angle>5)
        angle=angle+5
    Else if (angle>2)
        angle=angle+10
    Else
        angle=angle+15
    ```
    A. 35
    B. 25
    C. 15
    D. None of the above

16. Reference parameters
    A. are specified by using an & in the formal parameter list
    B. efficiently share complex objects with a function
    C. are used to pass back value from a function
    D. all of the above

17. Dynamic memory allocation occurs
    A. when a new variable is created by the complier
    B. when a new variable is created at runtime
    C. both A and B
    D. none of the above

18. What is the output of the following code?
    ```
    If ('A'=='A')&&('B'=='B')&&('C'=='C')
        Cout<<"equal";
    Else
        Cout<<"not equal";
    ```
    A. Equal
    B. Not equal
    C. Wrong code

Questions 19-21.

DIRECTIONS: Questions 19 through 21 are to be answered on the basis of the following figure.

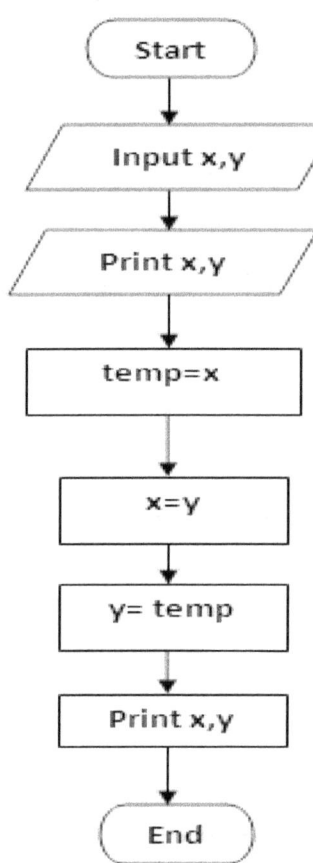

19. The flowchart represents the following problem:
    A. Swapping the two numbers
    B. Finding the average of three variables A, B and temp
    C. Finding lowest among x, y and temp
    D. none of the above

    19._____

20. What will be the output of this program?
    A. Compare two
    B. Values of x and y are exchanged
    C. Least number
    D. Stop

    20._____

21. In the flowchart, the parallelogram symbol indicates
    A. process
    B. condition
    C. input/output
    D. start

    21._____

5 (#1)

22. The diagrammatical representation of any operation that explains the sequence of actions to be performed to reach the solutions of any problem is called
    A. algorithm
    B. flowchart
    C. puesdocode
    D. programming

22.____

23. Int x = -1, y = 0
    While(x<=3)
    { y=y+2;
      X=x+1;
    }
    Cout<<y;
    What is the output of the above code?
    A. 10
    B. 11
    C. 9

23.____

24. _____ is a control structure that causes a statement or group of statements to repeat.
    A. Decision statement
    B. Loop
    C. Sequential structure

24.____

25. A counter can be defined as
    A. final value of a loop
    B. a variable that counts loop iteration
    C. the initial value of a loop

25.____

KEY (CORRECT ANSWERS)

1.	B		11.	A
2.	B		12.	D
3.	B		13.	A
4.	A		14.	B
5.	C		15.	C
6.	C		16.	D
7.	B		17.	B
8.	B		18.	B
9.	C		19.	A
10.	B		20.	B

21. C
22. B
23. A
24. B
25. B

TEST 2

DIRECTIONS: Each question or incomplete statement is followed by several suggested answers or completions. Select the one that BEST answers the question or completes the statement. *PRINT THE LETTER OF THE CORRECT ANSWER IN THE SPACE AT THE RIGHT.*

1. Formal parameters are also called _____ arguments.
   A. dummy   B. actual   C. original   D. referenced

2. The constructor of any class is called when
   A. function is called
   B. an object needs a destructor
   C. possible
   D. an object is created

3. Binary tree can be divided into
   A. leaves
   B. branches
   C. sub trees
   D. none of the above

4. Each node in a binary tree has
   A. exactly one child
   B. exactly two children
   C. almost two children
   D. none of the above

5. When functions Seekg and Seekp in C++ may have two arguments, then the first argument is the offset and the second argument may be _____ to indicate the base for the offset.
   A. ios::beg   B. ios::end   C. ios::cur   D. all

6. The MOST difficult part of problem solving is
   A. designing algorithm
   B. testing program
   C. documentation
   D. program execution

7. Given that x is a float variable and num is an int variable containing the value 38, what will x contain after execution of the following statement: x = num/4+3.0?
   A. 12.5   B. 13   C. 12   D. 12.0

8. How many bytes are occupied by float a, b?
   A. 1
   B. 8
   C. 16
   D. None of the above

9. The average and best-case complexity of Quick Sort is
   A. O(n)
   B. O(log n)
   C. O(n2)
   D. none of the above

10. What will strcmp ("Astring", "Astring"): return?
    A. A positive value
    B. A negative value
    C. Zero
    D. Something else

11. A static variable is used to
    A. make a variable visible to only one file of a program
    B. keep/conserve memory when a function is not executing
    C. retain a value of local variable of a function when it is not executing
    D. make a variable to keep for the entire routine of program

12. When an array argument is passed, what is actually passed?
    A. The address of the array
    B. The element of the array
    C. The number of elements of the array
    D. All of the above

13. If two pointer variables point to the same memory location, what happens when one of the pointers is freed?
    A. The other pointer should be considered to be un-initialized
    B. The other pointer still points to a valid memory address
    C. If you attempt to free the other pointer, a runtime error will occur
    D. A and C

14. Which of the following is TRUE about a constructor?
    A. A constructor cannot have parameter
    B. A constructor has the same name as class
    C. A class can only have a single constructor
    D. None of the above

15. int v=1; int v2 = -1; int*p1; int*p2,
    p1 = &v1;
    p2 = &v2;
    p2 = p1
    Cout <<*p2<<endl;
    What will be the output of the above code?
    A. 2   B. -1   C. -2   D. 1

16. The _____ function is used to append the specified number of characters of one string to end of second string.
    A. strncat()   B. Strchr()   C. Getch()   D. Strcspn()

17. Which has the highest precedence?
    A. ++   B. &&   C. || D. All are equal

18. In C++, the condition (7>x>3)
    A. evaluates correctly and could be replaced by (7>x&&x>3)
    B. does not evaluate correctly and should be replaced by (7>x&&x>3)
    C. evaluates correctly
    D. none of the above

Questions 19-20.

DIRECTIONS: Questions 19 and 20 are to be answered on the basis of the following figure.

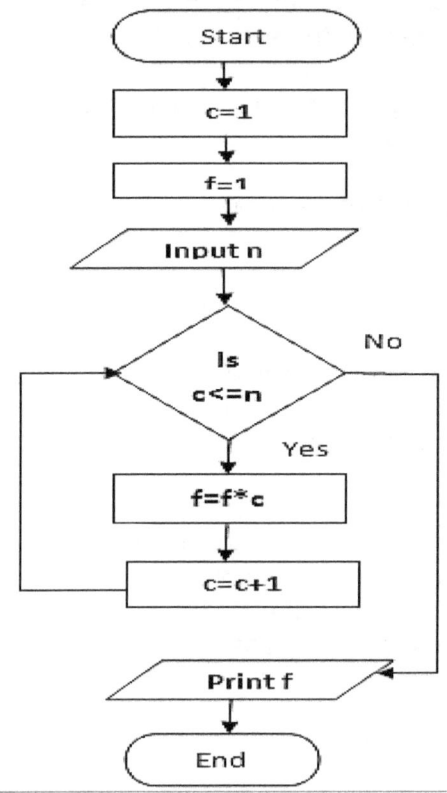

19. The flowchart represents the following problem: 19.____
    A. Finding the factorial of input number
    B. Finding largest among inputs
    C. Square of any number
    D. None of the above

20. What will be the output of this program? 20.____
    A. Generates the multiple of n numbers
    B. Factorial of any number
    C. Square of any number
    D. No output

21. In a flowchart, the terminator symbol indicates 21.____
    A. condition				B. start and stop
    C. process				D. documentation

22. ```
    int s=0, n=0
    do
    {n++;
      s+=n;
    if (s>=4) continue;
    }
      while (n<5);
    ```
    What will be the value of variable s after the above loop termination?
    A. 15   B. 14   C. 16   D. 18

    22.____

23. Which sort is adequate for searching through small arrays?
    A. Linear search   B. Binary search
    C. Forward search   D. Bubble sort

    23.____

24. An actor might be in UML
    A. different system that interacts with the system being used
    B. the designer of the system
    C. a software entity that helps the developer solve a particular coding program
    D. A and B
    E. none of the above

    24.____

25. To define class objects in different files, in each file you must
    A. declare the class   B. define the class
    C. declare the class using extern   D. define the class using extern

    25.____

KEY (CORRECT ANSWERS)

1.	A		11.	D
2.	D		12.	C
3.	C		13.	D
4.	B		14.	B
5.	D		15.	A
6.	A		16.	A
7.	D		17.	A
8.	B		18.	B
9.	B		19.	A
10.	C		20.	B

21.	B
22.	A
23.	A
24.	D
25.	B
    ```

TEST 3

DIRECTIONS: Each question or incomplete statement is followed by several suggested answers or completions. Select the one that BEST answers the question or completes the statement. *PRINT THE LETTER OF THE CORRECT ANSWER IN THE SPACE AT THE RIGHT.*

1. A queue is a data structure that stores and retrieves items in this manner. 1.____
   A. Last in, first out
   B. First in, last out
   C. First in, first out
   D. None of the above

2. Which function is used to compare the specified number of characters in the two strings? 2.____
   A. Strncmp
   B. Strchr
   C. Strcompare
   D. None of the above

3. The two-dimensional array of characters can contain 3.____
   A. strings of the same length
   B. uninitialized elements
   C. strings of different lengths
   D. none of the above

4. Which answer is MOST accurate for the statement a = *ptr_m? 4.____
   A. The variable must be a pointer.
   B. The value of variable that ptr_m is pointing to is being assigned to the variable a.
   C. The value of the pointer ptr_m is being assigned to the variable a.
   D. The address of pointer ptr_m is being assigned to the variable a.

5. Which of the following assign the fifth element of n array pointed to by a pointer P1 to the value 6? 5.____
   A. (p1+4)=6   B. (*p1)+4=6   C. *(p1+4)=6   D. *(p[4])=6

6. int a[] = [1,2,3,4,5,6,7,8,9] 6.____
   int*b;
   int*c = &(a[1]);
   b=a;
   b[2]=0;
   Cout«b[1]«c[0]«c[1]«a[2],,endl;
   What will be the output of the above code?
   A. 1345   B. 2200   C. 2378   D. 9789

7. Suppose that p1 and p2 are both pointers to the same integer variable x; y is another integer variable. After the execution of which of the statements below is the pointer variable p1 considered a dangling pointer? 7.____
   A. x=0   B. p1=&y   C. Delete x   D. Delete p2

8. Constructor for a class is called when 8.____
   A. a function is called
   B. an object needs a destructor
   C. an object is created
   D. none of the above

9. When a member function is defined outside the a class declaration, in its header the function name is preceded by the class name and
   A. extractor operator
   B. constructor function
   C. scope resolution operator
   D. none of the above

9.____

10. Which function is used to search a string for the first occurrence of a character belonging to the set of character in the second string?
    A. Strncat()   B. Strchr()   C. Getch()   D. Strcspn()

10.____

11. An array is passed to a function _____ and elements of an array are passed by _____.
    A. always by value; reference
    B. always by reference; value
    C. by reference; reference
    D. none of the above

11.____

12. The modulus operator is used for
    A. integer remainder
    B. multiplication
    C. division

12.____

Questions 13-14.

DIRECTIONS: Questions 13 and 14 are to be answered on the basis of the following flowchart.

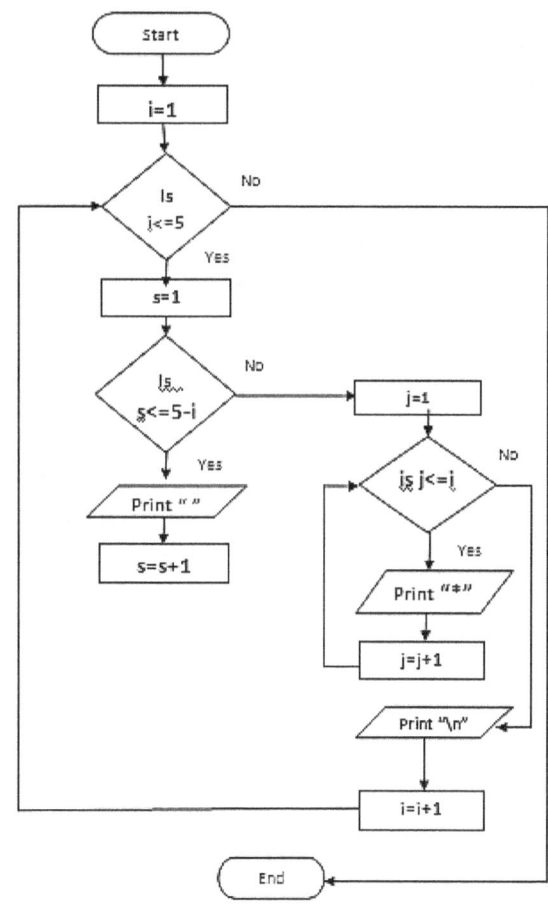

13. What will be the possible output of this flow diagram?   13._____

    A. * * * * *
        * * * *
        * * *
        * *
        *

    B. (diamond/rhombus shape made of asterisks)

    C.   *
              * *
            * * *
          * * * *
        * * * * *

    D. * * * * *
        * * * * *
        * * * * *
        * * * * *
        * * * * *

14. What will be the BEST choice of loop for the above flowchart?   14._____
    A. Nested for loop   B. For loop with nest do while
    C. Series of if structure   D. Switch statements

15. Page off page connector is used   15._____
    A. when a flowchart ends on one page and begins again on another page
    B. two or three flow lines are used to exit from decision symbol
    C. to represent an operation
    D. none of the above

16. int n=8;   16._____
    for (int i=1; i<=n*3; i++)
        n++;
    What will be the output of the above code?
    A. Infinite loop   B. 9   C. 12   D. 16

17. Suppose we do not have any other data structure like array & linked list,   17._____
    then what will be the total number of queues required to implement the stack?
    A. 2   B. 1   C. 4   D. 5

18. A sub class inherits all of the following members of its super class EXCEPT   18._____
    A. constructors and destructors   B. public methods
    C. data fields   D. protected methods

19.
```
              70
             /  \
            4    55
           / \    \
          2   7    36
             / \   /
            3  17 26
               /
              11
```
What is the post order traversal of the above binary search tree?
A. 2, 3, 11, 17, 7, 3, 26, 36, 55, 70
B. 11, 3, 2, 17, 7, 4, 26, 36, 55, 70
C. 2, 3, 11, 26, 36, 55, 70, 17, 7, 4
D. None of the above

20. Time complexity of post traversal BST is
A. O(n)
B. O(log n)
C. O(n2)
D. none of the above

21. In a sequence diagram of UML,
A. time goes from left to right
B. horizontal arrows represent messages
C. vertical dotted lines represent lifetime
D. both B and C

22. Assume there is an association between class A and class B. Also, OjbA is an object of class A and ObjB is the object of class B. Which of the following applies?
A. Obj A may send a message to Obj B
B. Class B must be a subclass of class A
C. Obj B may help obj A carry out a task
D. Both A and C

23. A method used to collect the information from all people of organization is
A. questionnaire
B. observation
C. sampling
D. all of the above

24. The total number of swap functions for complete execution selection sort algorithm of n elements is
A. 1
B. n-1
C. n log n
D. n^2

25. In a graph, if e=[u,v], then u and v are called   25.____
    A. neighbors   B. endpoints of e
    C. all nodes adjacent   D. above all

KEY (CORRECT ANSWERS)

1. C
2. A
3. D
4. B
5. C

6. B
7. D
8. C
9. C
10. D

11. A
12. A
13. C
14. A
15. A

16. A
17. A
18. D
19. A
20. A

21. D
22. D
23. A
24. B
25. D

TEST 4

DIRECTIONS: Each question or incomplete statement is followed by several suggested answers or completions. Select the one that BEST answers the question or completes the statement. *PRINT THE LETTER OF THE CORRECT ANSWER IN THE SPACE AT THE RIGHT.*

1. Int x=1, y=2, z=3;
   If ((x==y) || (y==z) || (z==2)
      Cout<<"yes";
   Else
      Cout<<"NO";
   What will be the output?
   A. Yes
   B. No
   C. Runtime error
   D. Zero

   1.____

2. Class method definition in UML
   A. should be placed in a header file
   B. should not be placed in a header file
   C. A and B
   D. none of the above

   2.____

3. The waterfall process
   A. consists of distinct phases
   B. was never actually used
   C. became untenable because of water storage

   3.____

4. A pure virtual class is a virtual function which
   A. causes its class to be abstract
   B. takes on arguments
   C. is used in a base class
   D. both A and C

   4.____

5. If p is Boolean variable, which of the following logical expressions always has the value false?
   A. p&&p
   B. p || p
   C. p &&!p
   D. p || !p

   5.____

6. Change into pre order traversal of this post order traversal of a binary tree:
   <u>L M J N K I</u>.
   A. IJNKLM
   B. ILJNMK
   C. IJLMKN
   D. IJLKMN

   6.____

7. When a derived class has two or more classes, the situation is known as
   A. multiple inheritance
   B. polymorphism
   C. access specification
   D. none of the above

   7.____

8. Two-dimensional arrays are called
   A. table
   B. matrix
   C. string
   D. both A and B

   8.____

9. Link list START=NULL
   A. Saturated
   B. Underflow
   C. Overflow
   D. None of the above

   9.____

33

Questions 10-11.

DIRECTIONS: Questions 10 and 11 are to be answered on the basis of the following flowchart.

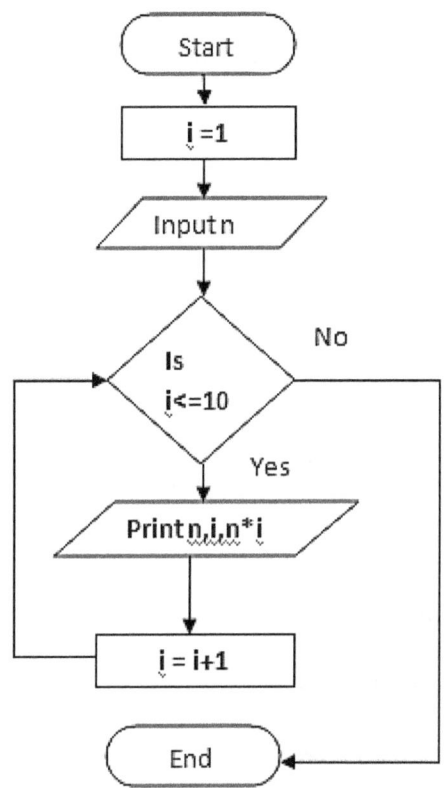

10. What will be the possible output of this flowchart? 10.____
    A. Finding largest among inputs
    B. Generate the table of input number
    C. Generate the square of any number
    D. None of the above

11. What will be the output of this program? 11.____
    A. Finding largest among inputs
    B. Generate the square of any number
    C. Generate the table of input number
    D. No output

12. The rectangle symbol in a flowchart indicates 12.____
    A. process   B. decision
    C. termination   D. none of the above

13. Complied program typically executes faster because
    A. complied programs are read and executed a line at a time
    B. complied programs are already in machine-readable form
    C. complied programs do not require any data
    D. none of the above

14. In C++, an STL algorithm is a
    A. stand-alone function that operates on containers
    B. link between member functions and containers
    C. friend function of an appropriate container class
    D. member function of an appropriate container class

15. In the unified process, which of the following happen from time to time?
    A. A use case diagram will be drawn up before the users have specified all the use cases.
    B. Some code will be written before the class diagram is complete.
    C. The header file with the class declaration will be changed while methods are still coded.
    D. All of the above

16. In deque,
    A. data can be inserted or deleted at any location, but the process is quite slow.
    B. insertion or deletion can be done quickly at any end
    C. insertion or deletion can be done at any end, but the process is quite slow
    D. A and B
    E. none of the above

17. Actual code for template class is generated when
    A. the function declaration appears in the source code
    B. the function definition appears in the source code
    C. a call to the function appears in the source code
    D. function is executed at runtime

18. A template class is shown in the UML as
    A. an ordinary class with something added
    B. a dashed line
    C. a rectangle with dashed line
    D. none of the above

19. The scope resolution operator usually
    A. limits the visibility if a variable to a certain function
    B. tells what base class a class is derived from
    C. specifies a particular class and resolves ambiguities
    D. none of the above

20. This statement can be used to stop a loop's current iteration?
    A. Continue   B. Break
    C. Semicolon   D. None of the above

21. What is the opposite of the Boolean expression (1<x&&x<100)? 21.____
    A. (x<=1 || 100<=x)   B. !((1<x&&x<100)
    C. Both A and B   D. None of the above

22. The document that explains the features of software and the way it is used 22.____
    is called
    A. software requirement specification   B. problem description
    C. user manual   D. algorithm

23. Cause and effect analysis is performed during 23.____
    A. logical design phase   B. problem analysis
    C. scope definition phase

24. Int x; 24.____
    A function (3,x)
    Void a function (int a, int &b)
    {
      b = a*5+1;
    }
    What is the value of x after the above function call?
    A. 16   B. 32   C. 14   D. 10

25. If y is 10 and z is 4? 25.____
    Switch(y-z)
    {   Case 8 x=y+2; break
         Case 9 x=y; break;
         Case 10 x=z; break;
         Default x=y*2;
    }
       A. 40   B. 42   C. 35   D. 45

KEY (CORRECT ANSWERS)

1. B
2. B
3. A
4. D
5. C

6. C
7. A
8. D
9. B
10. B

11. C
12. A
13. C
14. A
15. D

16. D
17. C
18. A
19. C
20. B

21. C
22. C
23. B
24. A
25. A

EXAMINATION SECTION
TEST 1

DIRECTIONS: Each question or incomplete statement is followed by several suggested answers or completions. Select the one that BEST answers the question or completes the statement. *PRINT THE LETTER OF THE CORRECT ANSWER IN THE SPACE AT THE RIGHT.*

1. In programming, declaring a variable name involves what else other than naming?
   A. Type   B. Length   C. Size   D. Style

2. Name of a student is an example of
   A. operation
   C. attribute
   B. method
   D. none of the above

3. Basic strength of a computer is
   A. speed   B. memory   C. accuracy   D. reliability

4. *Only girls can become members of the committee. Many of the members of the committee are officers. Some of the officers have been invited for dinner.* Based on the above statements, which is the CORRECT conclusion?
   A. All members of the committee have been invited for the dinner.
   B. Some officers are not girls.
   C. All girls are the members of the committee.
   D. None of the above

5. Of the following statements, which of them cannot both be true and both be false?
   I. All babies cry
   II. Some babies cry
   III. No babies cry
   IV. Some babies do not cry

   The CORRECT answer is:
   A. I and II   B. I and III   C. III and IV   D. I and IV

6. 3, 7, 15, 31, 63, ? What number should come next?
   A. 83   B. 127   C. 122   D. 76

7. If 30% of a number is 12.6, find the number?
   A. 45   B. 42   C. 54   D. 60

8. 10, 25, 45, 54, 60, 75, 80. The odd one out is
   A. 10   B. 45   C. 54   D. 60

9. Complement of an input is produced by which logical function?
   A. AND   B. OR   C. NOT   D. XOR

10. *If marks are greater than 70 and less than 85, then the grade is B.* 10.____
    This statement is an example of which programming control structure?
    A. Decision
    B. Loop
    C. Sequence
    D. None of the above

11. In programming, which operator is called the assignment operator? 11.____
    A. +   B. =   C. _   D. %

12. In programming, which operator is called the modulus operator? 12.____
    A. +   B. =   C. %   D. /

13. What is the correct order of running a computer program? 13.____
    A. Linking, loading, execution, translation
    B. Loading, translation, execution, linking
    C. Execution, translation, linking, loading
    D. Translation, loading, linking, execution

14. In the case of structure of programming, which of the following terms means "if none of the other statements are true"? 14.____
    A. Else   B. Default   C. While   D. If

15. True statements: 15.____
    i. All benches are chairs.
    ii. Some chairs are desks.
    iii. All desks are pillars.
    Conclusions:
    I. Some pillars are benches.
    II. Some pillars are chairs.
    III. Some desks are benches.
    IV. No pillar is a bench.

    The CORRECT answer is:
    A. None of the above
    B. Either I or IV, and III
    C. Either I or IV
    D. Either I or IV, and II
    E. All of the above

16. True statements: 16.____
    i. Some snakes are reptiles.
    ii. All reptiles are poisonous.
    iii. Some poisonous reptiles are not snakes.
    Conclusions:
    I. Some poisonous reptiles are snakes.
    II. All snakes are poisonous.
    III. All reptiles are snakes.
    IV. No poisonous reptile is a snake.

    The CORRECT answer is:
    A. None of the above
    B. Either I or IV, and III
    C. Either I or IV, and II
    D. All of the above

17. Anna runs faster than Peter.
    Jane runs faster than Anna.
    Peter runs faster than Jane.
    If the first two statements are true, the third statement would be
    A. true   B. false   C. unknown   D. both

18. The sum of the digits of a two-digit number is 10. If the new number formed by reversing the digits is greater than the original number by 36, then what will be the original number?
    A. 37   B. 39   C. 57   D. 28

19. If an inverter is added to the output of an AND gate, what logic function is produced?
    A. AND   B. NAND   C. XOR   D. OR

20. Decimal 7 is represented by which gray code?
    A. 0111   B. 1011   C. 0100   D. 0101

21. According to propositional logic, if p = "A car costs less than $20,000", q = "David will buy a car."
    p → ~q refers to which of the following?
    A. If David will buy a car, the car costs less than $20,000.
    B. David will not buy a car if the car costs less than $20,000.
    C. David will buy a car if the car costs less than $20,000.
    D. None of the above

22. Which Boolean algebra rule is wrong?
    A. 0 + A = A   B. 0 + A = 1   C. A + A = A
    D. x • 1 = 1   E. All of the above

23. The 2's complement of 001011 is
    A. 110101   B. 010101   C. 110100   D. 010100

24. 7, 10, 8, 11, 9, 12. What number should come next?
    A. 12   B. 13   C. 8   D. 10

25. 2, 1, (1/2), (1/4). What number should come next?
    A. (1/16)   B. (1/8)   C. (2/8)   D. 1

KEY (CORRECT ANSWERS)

1.	A		11.	B
2.	C		12.	C
3.	B		13.	D
4.	D		14.	B
5.	B		15.	C
6.	B		16.	C
7.	B		17.	B
8.	C		18.	A
9.	C		19.	B
10.	A		20.	C

21. B
22. B
23. A
24. D
25. B

———

TEST 2

DIRECTIONS: Each question or incomplete statement is followed by several suggested answers or completions. Select the one that BEST answers the question or completes the statement. *PRINT THE LETTER OF THE CORRECT ANSWER IN THE SPACE AT THE RIGHT.*

1. 8, 27, 64, 100, 125, 216, 343. The odd one out is 1.____
   A. 343 B. 8 C. 27 D. 100

2. In programming, what is the operator precedence? 2.____
   A. Arithmetic, comparison, logical
   B. Comparison, arithmetic, logical
   C. Arithmetic, logical, comparison
   D. Logical, arithmetic, comparison

3. Which of the following is NOT a type of programming error? 3.____
   A. Logical B. Syntax C. Superficial D. Runtime

4. Statements: 4.____
   i. No man is good. ii. Jack is a man.
   Conclusions:
   I. Jack is not good II. All men are not Jack.

   The CORRECT answer is:
   A. I B. II
   C. Either I or II D. Neither I nor II
   E. Both I and II

5. Statements: 5.____
   i. All students are boys. ii. No boy is dull.
   Conclusions:
   I. There are no girls in the class. II. No student is dull.

   The CORRECT answer is:
   A. I B. II
   C. Either I or II D. Neither I nor II
   E. Both I and II

6. What is the sum of two consecutive even numbers, the difference of whose squares is 84? 6.____
   A. 32 B. 36 C. 40 D. 42

7. Choose the odd one out:

   A. 1   B. 2   C. 3   D. 4

8. In the Netherlands, almost 200 cyclists die each year on the road.
   Head injury is the main cause of death among cyclists.
   Which of the following statements is true based on the above information?
   A. In the Netherlands, if wearing a helmet was widespread among cyclists, the number of deaths in cyclists could be reduced.
   B. Too many cyclists die each year on the road in the Netherlands.
   C. Most deaths in the Netherlands occur due to cycling.
   D. None of the above

9. According to propositional logic, what is the order of precedence of operators?
   A. ^, v, ↔, →
   B. ~, ^, v, →, ↔
   C. ~, v, ^, ↔, →
   D. →, ~, ^, v, ↔

10. The binary equivalent of the number 50 is
    A. 01101   B. 11010   C. 11100   D. 110010

11. Number 200 can be represented by how many bits?
    A. 1   B. 5   C. 8   D. 10

12. Which of the following is NOT true?
    A. 0 × 0 = 0   B. 1 × 0 = 0   C. 0 × 1 = 1   D. 1 × 1 = 1

13. Get two numbers
    If first number is bigger than second then
    Print first number
    Else
    Print second number
    The above pseudo-code is an example of which control structure?
    A. Loop
    B. Sequence
    C. Decision
    D. None of the above

14. A group of variables is called
    A. data structure
    B. control structure
    C. data object
    D. linked list

15. The first character of the string variable St is represented by
    A. St[1]
    B. St[0]
    C. St
    D. none of the above

16. Statements:
    i. No girl is poor B. All girls are rich
    Conclusions:
    I. No poor girl is rich II. No rich girl is poor

    The CORRECT answer is:
    A. I B. II
    C. Either I or II D. Neither I nor II
    E. Both I and II

17. Statements:
    i. All fishes are orange in color ii. Some fishes are heavy
    Conclusions:
    I. All heavy fishes are orange in color
    II. All light fishes are not orange in color

    The CORRECT answer is:
    A. I B. II
    C. Either I or II D. Neither I nor II
    E. Both I and II

18. 3, 7, 6, 5, 9, 3, 12, 1, 15. What number should come next?
    A. 18 B. 13 C. 1 D. -1

19. 5184, 1728, 576, 192. What number should come next?
    A. 64 B. 32 C. 120 D. 44

20. $(p \Leftrightarrow r) \Rightarrow (q \Leftrightarrow r)$ is equivalent to
    A. $[(\sim p \lor r) \land (p \lor \sim r)] \lor \sim [(\sim q \lor r) \land (q \lor \sim r)]$
    B. $\sim[(\sim p \lor r) \land (p \lor \sim r)] \lor [(\sim q \lor r) \land (q \lor \sim r)]$
    C. $[(\sim p \lor r) \land (p \lor \sim r)] \land [(\sim q \lor r) \land (q \lor \sim r)]$
    D. $[(\sim p \lor r) \land (p \lor \sim r)] \lor [(\sim q \lor r) \land (q \lor \sim r)]$

21. Which of the following propositions is a tautology?
    A. $(p \lor q) \rightarrow q$ B. $p \lor (q \rightarrow p)$ C. $p \lor (p \rightarrow q)$ D. b & c

22. According to propositional logic, if p = "Mary gets an A in computer science", q = "Mary got 90% marks in computer science."
    p ↔ q refers to which of the following?
    A. Mary gets an A in computer science if and only if her percentage in computer science is 90%.
    B. Mary might get an A in computer science if her percentage in computer science is 90%
    C. Mary get an A in computer science if her percentage in computer science is 90%.
    D. None of the above

23. What does the following flowchart depict?   23._____

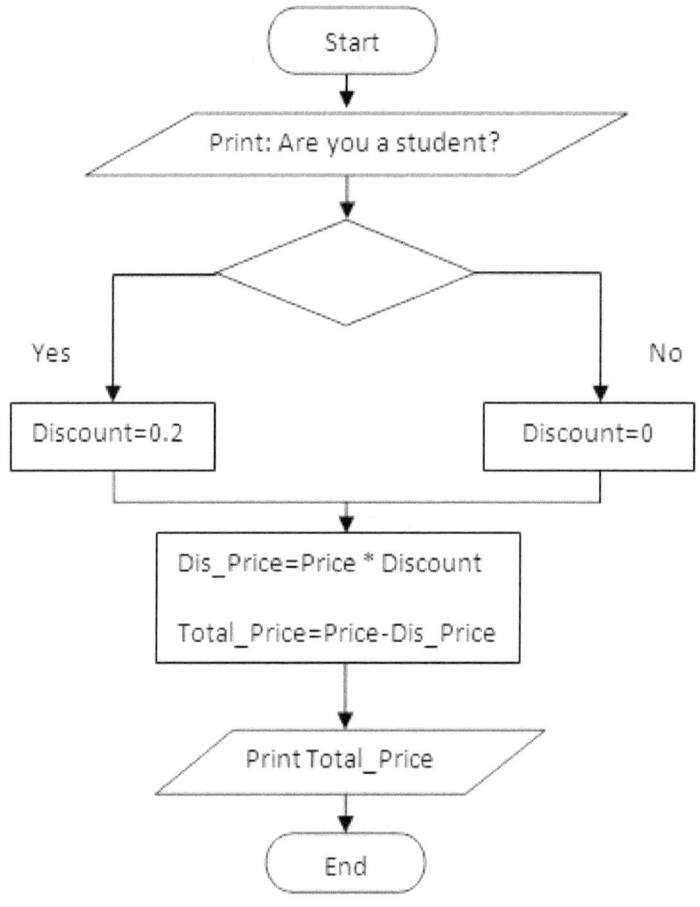

A. All users get a discount.
B. If user is a student, only then does he get a discount.
C. If user is a student, he does not get a discount, while other users get a discount.
D. None of the above

24. 13, 35, 57, 79, 911. What number should come next?   24._____
    A. 1113   B. 1114   C. 1100   D. 1111

25. Choose the missing shape.

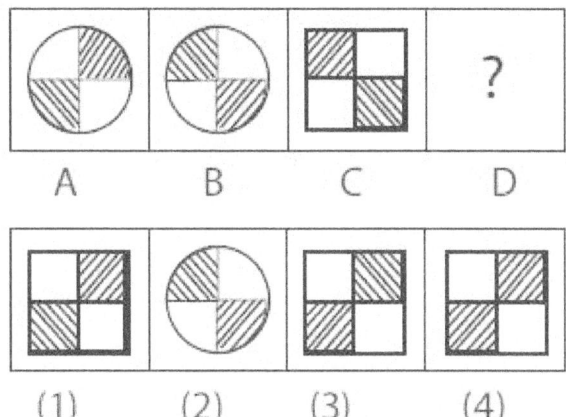

A. 1   B. 2   C. 3   D. 4

KEY (CORRECT ANSWERS)

1. D
2. A
3. C
4. A
5. E

6. D
7. A
8. A
9. B
10. D

11. C
12. C
13. C
14. A
15. B

16. E
17. A
18. D
19. A
20. B

21. D
22. A
23. B
24. C
25. C

TEST 3

DIRECTIONS: Each question or incomplete statement is followed by several suggested answers or completions. Select the one that BEST answers the question or completes the statement. *PRINT THE LETTER OF THE CORRECT ANSWER IN THE SPACE AT THE RIGHT.*

1. The following flowchart represents which control structure? 1.____

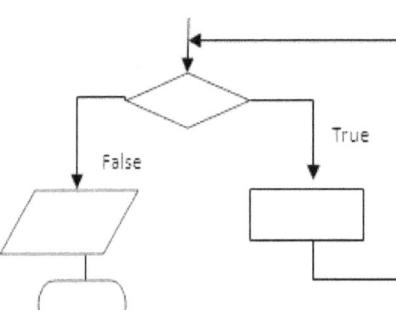

   A. If/else   B. For   C. While   D. Switch

2. The processing steps of a program are grouped into a set of related programming statements called 2.____
    A. components
    B. objects
    C. modules
    D. none of the above

3. Statements: 3.____
    i. Some engineers are intelligent
    ii. Some intelligent are poor
    Conclusions:
    I. Some engineers are poor
    II. Some poor are engineers

    The CORRECT answer is:
    A. I
    B. II
    C. Either I or II
    D. Neither I nor II
    E. Both I and II

4. Statements: 4.____
    i. No man is a fool
    ii. John is a man
    Conclusions:
    I. John is not a fool
    II. All men are not John

    The CORRECT answer is:
    A. I
    B. II
    C. Either I or II
    D. Neither I nor II
    E. Both I and II

5. John weighs less than Fred.
   John weighs more than Boomer.
   Of the three dogs, Boomer weighs the least.

   If the first two statements are true, the third statement is
   A. true   B. false   C. uncertain   D. both

6. A file contains 10 sheets and none of these sheets is blue. Which of the following statements can be deduced?
   A. None of the 10 sheets contained in the file are blue.
   B. The file contains a blue sheet.
   C. The file contains at least one yellow sheet.
   D. None of the above

7. Choose the odd one out:

   (1)   (2)   (3)   (4)

   A. 1   B. 2   C. 3   D. 4

8. Which of the following structures requires the statements to be repeated until a condition is met?
   A. Sequence   B. If….Else
   C. For   D. None of the above

9. While n is greater than 0
   Increment count
   end
   The above pseudo-code represents which programming structure?
   A. Sequence   B. Loop
   C. Structure   D. None of the above

10. Which of the following converts a source code into machine code and turns it into an exe file?
    A. Linker   B. Compiler
    C. Interpreter   D. None of the above

11. Which of the following is used to hide data and its functionality?
    A. Structure   B. Loop
    C. Object   D. Selection statement

12. Statements:
    i. All apples are golden in color
    ii. No golden colored things are cheap
    Conclusions:
    I. All apples are cheap
    II. Golden colored apples are not cheap

    The CORRECT answer is:
    A. I
    B. II
    C. Either I or II
    D. Neither I nor II
    E. Both I and II

13. Statements:
    i. All cups are glasses
    ii. All glasses are bowls
    iii. No bowl is a plate
    Conclusions:
    I. No cup is a plate
    II. No glass is a plate
    III. Some plates are bowls
    IV. Some cups are not glasses

    The CORRECT answer is:
    A. None of the above
    B. Either I or IV, and III
    C. Either I or IV
    D. Either I or IV, and II
    E. All of the above

14. 331, 482, 551, 263, 383, 362, 284. The odd one out is
    A. 331   B. 383   C. 284   D. 551

15. 3, 5, 7, 12, 17, 19. The odd one out is
    A. 7   B. 17   C. 12   D. 19

16. Ratio of 12 minutes to 1 hour is:
    A. 2:3   B. 1:5   C. 1:6   D. 1:8

17. 10 cats caught 10 rats in 10 seconds. How many cats are required to catch 100 rats in 100 seconds?
    A. 100   B. 50   C. 200   D. 10

18. Four engineers and six technicians can complete a project in 8 days, while three engineers and seven technicians can complete it in 10 days. In how many days will ten technicians complete it?
    A. 40   B. 36   C. 50   D. 45

19. According to propositional logic, if p = "Jane is smart", "q = "Jane is honest", then p v (~p ^ q) refers to which of the following?
    A. Either Jane is smart or honest.
    B. Jane is smart and honest.
    C. Either Jane is smart, or she is not smart but honest.
    D. None of the above

20. In binary number system, the number 102 is equal to 20._____
    A. 1100110   B. 1001100   C. 1110110   D. 1100101

21. In base 8, number 362 is represented as 21._____
    A. 550   B. 552   C. 545   D. 566

22. 396, 462, 572, 427, 671, 264. The odd one out is 22._____
    A. 427   B. 572   C. 671   D. 264

23. A is two years older than B who is twice as old as C. If the total of the ages of A, B and C is 27, then how old is B? 23._____
    A. 10   B. 11   C. 12   D. 13

24. What is 50% of 40% of Rs. 3,450? 24._____
    A. 580   B. 670   C. 690   D. 570

25. What is the minimum number of colors required to fill the spaces in the following diagram without the adjacent sides having the same color? 25._____

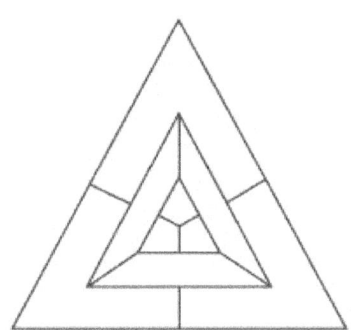

A. 3
C. 6
B. 4
D. Not possible to determine

KEY (CORRECT ANSWERS)

1.	A		11.	A
2.	C		12.	B
3.	E		13.	A
4.	A		14.	D
5.	A		15.	C
6.	A		16.	B
7.	D		17.	D
8.	C		18.	A
9.	B		19.	C
10.	B		20.	A

21. B
22. A
23. A
24. C
25. A

TEST 4

DIRECTIONS: Each question or incomplete statement is followed by several suggested answers or completions. Select the one that BEST answers the question or completes the statement. *PRINT THE LETTER OF THE CORRECT ANSWER IN THE SPACE AT THE RIGHT.*

1. Computer signals that include both measuring and counting are called 1.____
   A. analog B. digital
   C. hybrid D. none of the above

2. The result of ANDing 5 and 4 is 2.____
   A. 30 B. 9
   C. 20 D. none of the above

3. If one wants to trace an organization's purchase orders from creation to final disposition, he should use which of the following? 3.____
   A. Data flow diagram B. Internal control flow chart
   C. System flow chart D. Program flow chart

4. Statements: 4.____
   i. Some tables are sofas ii. All furniture are tables
   Conclusions:
   I. Some furniture are sofas II. Some sofas are furniture

   The two statements given should be assumed to be true. Select the conclusion.
   A. I B. II
   C. Either I or II D. Neither I nor II
   E. Both I and II

5. Statements: 5.____
   i. Many actors are singers. ii. All singers are dancers.
   Conclusions:
   I. Some actors are dancers. II. No singer is an actor.

   The CORRECT answer is:
   A. I B. II
   C. Either I or II D. Neither I nor II
   E. Both I and II

6. Anna will not pass both the verbal reasoning test and quantitative reasoning test. This statement refers to which of the following? 6.____
   A. Anna will not pass the verbal reasoning test.
   B. Anna will neither pass quantitative reasoning test nor verbal reasoning test.
   C. Anna will pass either the verbal reasoning test or the numerical reasoning test.
   D. If Anna passes the verbal reasoning test, she will not pass the numerical reasoning test.

7. Which symbol is used at the beginning of the flowchart?

   A. ○   B. ⬭   C. ◇   D. ▭

8. A list of instructions in a proper order to solve a problem is called
   A. sequence
   B. algorithm
   C. flowchart
   D. none of the above

9. Statements:
   i. Some pearls are stones
   ii. Some stones are diamonds
   iii. No diamond is a gem
   Conclusions:
   I. Some gems are pearls
   II. Some gems are diamonds
   III. No gem is a diamond
   IV. No gem is a pearl

   The CORRECT answer is:
   A. None of the above
   B. Either I or IV, and III
   C. Either I or IV
   D. Either I or IV, and II
   E. All of the above

10. 53, 53, 40, 40, 27, 27. What number should come next?
    A. 14   B. 12   C. 13   D. 10

11. 1, 3, 1, 9, 1, 81, 1. What number should come next?
    A. 4   B. 1   C. 343   D. 6561

12. A father is 30 years older than his son. He will be three times as old as his son after 5 years. What is the father's present age?
    A. 30   B. 35   C. 40   D. 45

13. Ahmed is older than Ali
    Maria is older than Ahmed.
    Ali is older than Maria.
    If the first two statements are true, the third statement is
    A. true   B. false   C. unknown   D. both

14. All flowers are fruit.
    Some flowers are leaves.
    All leaves are fruit.
    If the first two statements are true, the third statement is
    A. true   B. false   C. unknown   D. both

15. The Spring Mall has more stores than the Four Seasons Mall.
    The Four Corners Mall has fewer stores than the Four Seasons Mall.
    The Spring Mall has more stores than the Four Corners Mall.
    If the first two statements are true, the third statement is
    A. true   B. false   C. unknown   D. both

16. Choose the odd one out:

    (1)   (2)   (3)   (4)

    A. 1	B. 2	C. 3	D. 4

17. Fact 1: All cats like to jump.
    Fact 2: Some cats like to run.
    Fact 3: Some cats look like dogs.
    If the first three statements are true, which of the following statements must also be true?
    I. All cats who like to jump look like dogs.
    II. Cats who like to run also like to jump.
    III. Cats who like to jump do not look like dogs.

    The CORRECT answer is:
    A. I only	B. II only
    C. II and III only	D. None of the above

18. Fact 1: All chickens are birds.
    Fact 2: Some chickens are hens.
    Fact 3: Female birds lay eggs.
    If the first three statements are true, which of the following statements must also be true?
    I. All birds lay eggs.
    II. Some hens are birds.
    III. Some chickens are not hens.

    The CORRECT answer is:
    A. I only	B. II only
    C. II and III only	D. None of the above

19. Fact 1: Jake has four watches.
    Fact 2: Two of the watches are black.
    Fact 3: One of the watches is a Rolex.
    If the first three statements are true, which of the following statements must also be true?
    I. Jake has a Rolex.
    II. Jake has three watches.
    III. Jake's favorite color is black.

    The CORRECT answer is:
    A. I only	B. II only
    C. II and III only	D. None of the above

20. Which symbol of a flowchart is used to test a condition?   20.____

    A. ○   B. ▱   C. ◇   D. ⬭

21. Which symbol of a flowchart is used for input and output?   21.____

    A. ○   B. ▱   C. ◇   D. ▭

22. Which of the following is NOT one of the categories of flowcharting symbols?   22.____
    A. Input/output symbols   B. Processing symbols
    C. Storage symbols   D. Flow symbols

23. Choose the missing shape.   23.____

    A. 1   B. 2   C. 3   D. 4

24. Choose the missing shape.   24.____

    A. 1   B. 2   C. 3   D. 4

25. How many minimum numbers of colors will be required to fill a cube without adjacent sides having the same color?

  A. 3   B. 4   C. 6   D. 8

25._____

KEY (CORRECT ANSWERS)

1.	C	11.	D
2.	C	12.	C
3.	B	13.	B
4.	E	14.	C
5.	A	15.	A
6.	B	16.	A
7.	B	17.	B
8.	B	18.	B
9.	B	19.	A
10.	A	20.	C

21.	B
22.	C
23.	B
24.	A
25.	A

EXAMINATION SECTION

TEST 1

DIRECTIONS: Each question or incomplete statement is followed by several suggested answers or completions. Select the one that BEST answers the question or completes the statement. *PRINT THE LETTER OF THE CORRECT ANSWER IN THE SPACE AT THE RIGHT.*

1. Given the definition: string[] colors = {"alpha", "bravo", "Charlie"}; 1.____
   What will you get if you display the following on console?
   colors.max(c=>c.length);
   A. 3
   B. Alpha
   C. Charlie
   D. No output; it is a compilation error
   E. No output; an exception is thrown

2. ```
   class Bravo
   {
       static int s;
       public static void main(String [] args)
       {
           Bravo p = new Bravo();
           p.start();
           System.ot.println(s);
       }
       void start()
       {
           int x = 7;
           Doogna(x);
           System.ouit.print(x+ " ");
       }
       void Doogna(int x)
       {
           x = x*2;
           s = x;
       }
   }
   ```
   2.____

   Which of the following is the correct output for the above code?
   A. 7 7   B. 7 14   C. 14 0   D. 14 14
   ```

3.
```
public class OnOff2
{
final static shot x = 2;
public static int y = 0;
public static void main(String [] args)
{
        for (int z = 0; z < 3; z++)
        {
        OnOff(z)
        {
        case x: System.out.print("0");
        case x-1: System.out.print("1");
        case x-2: System.out.print("2");
        }
        }
    }
}
```
What will be the output of the above program?
A. 0 1 2 B. 0 1 2 1 2 2 C. 2 1 0 1 0 0 D. 2 1 2 0 1 2

3.____

4.
```
public class OnOff2
    {
        final static short x = 2;
        public static int y = 0;
        public static void main(String [] args
        {
            for (int z = 0; z < 3; z++)
            {
                OnOff(z)
                {
                    case y: System.out.print("0"); /*Line 21*/
                    case x-1: System.out.print("1"); /*Line 22*/
                    case x: System.out.print("2"); /*Line 23*/
                }
            }
        }
    }
```
What will be the output of the above program?
A. 0 1 2   B. 0 1 2 1 2 2
C. Compile error line 21   D. Compile error line 22

4.____

5.
```
public class OnOff2
{
    final static short x = 2;
    public static int y = 0
    public static void main(String [] args)
    {
        for(int z = 0; z < 4; z++)
        {
            OnOff(z)
            {
                case x: System.out.print("0");
                default: System.out.print("beep");
                case x-1: System.out.print("1");
                    break;
                case x-2: System.out.print("2");
            }
        }
    }
}
```
What will be the output of the above program?
- A. 0 beep 1
- B. 2 1 0 beep 1
- C. 2 1 0 beep beep
- D. 2 1 0 beep 1 beep 1

6.
```
public class Bravo
{
    public static void main(String args[])
    {
        String str = NULL;
        System.out.println(str);
    }
}
```
What will be the output of the above program?
- A. NULL
- B. Compile error
- C. No error no output
- D. Runtime exception

7. What will be the output of the program:
```
public class SyncBravo
{
    public static void main(String [] args)
    {
        Thread t = new Thread()
        {
            Foo f = new Foo();
            public void run()
            {
                f.increase(20);
            }
        };
        t.start();
    }
}
class Foo
{
    private int data = 23;
    public void increase(int amt)
    {
        int x = data;
        data = x + amt;
    }
}
```
Which of the following is a course of action you will adapt from the following to ensure data integrity?
   A. Synchronize the run method
   B. Synchronize the increase() method
   C. Maniplate f.increase()
   D. It will be a runtime exception

7.____

8.
```
class Bravo 116
{
static final MyBuffer mb1 = new MyBuffer();
static final MyBuffer mb2 = new MyBuffer();
public static void main(String args [])
{
    new Thread()
    {
        public void run()
        {
            synchronized(sb1)
            {
                mb1.append("A");
                mb2.append("B");
            }
        }
```

8.____

```
            }.start();
            new Thread()
            {
                public void run()
                {
                    synchronized(mb1)
                    {
                        mb1.append("C");
                        mb2.append("D");
                    }
                }
            }.start();
            System.out.println(mb1 + " " + mb2);
        }
    }
```
What will be the output of the above program?
- A. Main() ends before any thread initialization
- B. Main() ends during thread execution
- C. Main() ends after thread execution
- D. Unpredictable

9.
```
    public class Bravo
    {
        public static void main(String[] args)
        {
            int x = 0;
            assert (x>0): "assertion failed";
            System.out.println("finished");
        }
    }
```
What will be the output of the above program?
- A. Finished
- B. Compilation fails
- C. Error
- D. Error and output both

9.____

10.
```
    public class Bravo2
    {
        public static int x;
        public static int foo(int y)
        {
            return y*2;
        }
        public static void main(String [] args)
        {
            int z = 5;
            assert z>0; /*Line 31*/
            assert z>2: food(z);/*Line 32*/
            if (z<7)
                assert z> 4; /*Line 34*/
```

10.____

```
        OnOff(z)
        {
            case 4: System.out.println("4");
            case 5: System.out.println("5");
            default: assert z>10;
        }
        if(z<10)
            assert z>4; z++; /*Line 22*/
        System.out.println(z);
    }
}
```
Considering the above code snippet, refer to commented lines. Which line uses assertions?
  A. 31   B. 32   C. 34   D. 42

11. ```
    String x = "xyz";
    x.toUpperCase();
    String y = x.replace('Y','y');
    y = y + "abc";
    System.out.println(y);
    ```
    What will be the output of the above program?
      A. abcXyZ   B. abcxyz   C. xyzabc   D. XyZabc

12. ```
    class Human{}
    class Monkey extends Human {}
    class Ape extends Human {}
    public class Universe
    {
        public static void main (String [] args)
        {
            Human human = new Monkey();
            if(human instanceof Monkey)
                System.out.println ("Monkey");
            else if(human instanceof Human)
                System.out.println ("Human");
            else if(human instanceof Ape)
                System.out.println("Ape");
            else
                System.out.println("Naaa");
        }
    }
    ```
    What will be the output of the above program?
      A. Monkey   B. Human   C. Universe   D. Naaa

13. Assume variable below to be of type byte.
    Which option checks 4th bit from right to be on?
    A. if((n&16) = = 16)
        Console.WriteLine("Yes! this one");
    B. if((n&8) = = 8)
        Console.WriteLine("Yes! this one");
    C. if((n!8) = = 8)
        Console.WriteLine("Yes! this one");
    D. if ((n^8) = = 8)
        Console.WriteLine("Yes! this one");
    E. if((n~8) = = 8)
        Console.WriteLine("Yes! this one");

13.____

14. ```
    namespace IndiabixConsoleApplication
    {
        class SampleProgram
        {
            static void Main(string [] args)
            {
                int i  = 10;
                double d = 34.340;
                fun(i);
                fun(d);
            }
            static void fun(double d)
            {
                Console.WriteLine(d + " ");
            }
        }
    }
    ```
    What is the output of the above code snippet?
    A. 10.000000 34.340000   B. 10 34
    C. 10 34.340   D. 10 34.34

14.____

15. ```
    public class Bravo138
    {
        public static void stringReplace(String text)
        {
            text = text.replace('j', 'c');/*Line 5*/
        }
        public static void bufferReplace(MyBuffer text)
        {
            text = text.append("c"); /*Line 9*/
        }
        public static void main(String args [])
        {
    ```

15.____

```
        String textString = new String ("java");
        MyBuffer textBuffere = new MyBuffer ("java"); /*Line 14*/
        stringReplace(textStrinig);
        bufferReplace(textBuffer);
        System.out.println(textString + textBuffer);
    }
}
```
What will be the output of the above program?
   A. java   B. javac   C. javajavac   D. Compile error

16.
```
public class StringRef
{
    public static void main(String [] args)
    {
        String s1 = "abc";
        String s2 = "def";
        String s3 = s2; /*Line 7*/
        s2 = "ghi";
        System.out.println(s1+s2+s3);
    }
}
```
What will be the output of the above program?
   A. abcdefghi   B. abcdefdef   C. abcghidef   D. abcghighi

16.____

17.
```
interface Foo141
{
    int k = 0; /*Line 3*/
}
public class Bravo141 implements Foo141
{
    public static void main(String args [])
    {
        int i;
        Bravo141 Bravo141 = new Bravo141();
        i = Bravo141.k; /*Line 11*/
        i = Bravo141.k;
        i = Foo141.k;
    }
}
```
What will be the output of the above program?
   A. Compilation fails
   B. Compiles and runs ok
   C. Compiles but throws an Exception at runtime
   D. Compiles but throws a RuntimeException at runtime

17.____

18. String x = "xyz";
    x.toUpperCase(); /*Line 2*/
    String y = x.replace('Y', 'y');
    y = y + "abc";
    System.out.println(y);
    What will be the output of the above program?
    A. abcXyZ   B. abcxyz   C. xyzabc   D. XyZabc

    18.____

19. Which one of the following will declare an array and initialize it with five numbers?
    A. Array a = new Array(5);   B. int [] a = [23,22,21,20,19];
    C. int a [] = new int[5];   D. int [5] array;

    19.____

20. public class Bravo
    {
        public static void main(String [] args)
        {
            signed int x = 10;
            for(int y=0); y<5; y++, x--)
                System.out.print(x+ ",");
        }
    }
    What will be the output of the above program?
    A. 10, 9, 8, 7, 6,   B. 9, 8, 7, 6, 5,
    C. Compilation fails   D. An exception is thrown at runtime

    20.____

21. public class CommandArgsThree
    {
        public static void main(String [] args)
        {
            String [] [] argCopy = new String[2][2];
            int x;
            argCopy[0] = args;
            x = argCopy[0].length;
            for(int y=0; y<x; y++)
            {
                System.out.print(" " + argCopy[0][y]);
            }
        }
    }
    What will be the output of the above program?
    A. 0 0   B. 1 2   C. 0 0 0   D. 1 2 3

    21.____

22. ```
    class Bravo
    {
        static int s;
        public static void main(String [] args)
        {
            Bravo p = new Bravo();
            p.start();
            System.out.println(s);
        }
        void start()
        {
            int x = 7;
            Doogna(x);
            System.out.print(x + " ");
        }
        void Doogna(int x)
        {
            x = x*2;
            s = x;
        }
    }
    ```
    What will be the output of the above program?
    A. 7 7　　　　B. 7 14　　　　C. 14 0　　　　D. 14 14

22.____

23. short b1 = 2;
    short b2 = 5000;
    int a;
    a – b1*b2;
    Which of the following statements is CORRECT?
    A. The variable a is assigned a value of 10000.
    B. The variable a is negative.
    C. Value will wrap around.
    D. An error is generated due to no possible conversion.
    E. An overflow occurs beyond the range of integer values.

23.____

24. The procedure daisy() receives int, Single, and double returns a decimal. Which of the following is a way of achieving this?
    A. daisy(int i, Single j, double k) decimal
       {...}
    B. static decimal daisy(int i, Single j, double k)
       {...}
    C. daisy(int i, Single j, double k)
       {
           ...
           return decimal;
       }
    D. static decimal daisy(int i, Single j, double k) decimal
       {...}
    E. A procedure can never return a value

24.____
    ```

25. a and b both need to be assigned a value of 19.
    I.   int a = 19; int b = 19;
    II. int a, b;
         a = 19: b = 19;;
    III. int a = 19, b = 19;
    IV. int a, b = 19;
    V.   int a = b = 19;
    Which of the following could be a possible way of doing this?
        A. II, IV   B. I, III   C. III, V   D. IV, V

25.____

KEY (CORRECT ANSWERS)

1. A
2. B
3. D
4. C
5. D

6. B
7. B
8. D
9. B
10. D

11. C
12. A
13. C
14. D
15. C

16. C
17. B
18. C
19. B
20. C

21. D
22. B
23. A
24. E
25. B

EXAMINATION SECTION
TEST 1

DIRECTIONS: Each question or incomplete statement is followed by several suggested answers of completions. Select the one that best answers the question or Complete the statement. *PRINT THE LETTER OF THE CORRECT ANSWER IN THE SPACE AT THE RIGHT.*

1. In the OSI model, a hub is defined in which of the following layers? 1.____

    A. Session
    B. Application
    C. Data link
    D. Physical

2. A simple definition of bandwidth is the 2.____

    A. number of computers in a network
    B. transmission capacity
    C. classification of network IPs
    D. none of the above

3. _____ topology makes use of terminators. 3.____

    A. Star
    B. Ring
    C. Bus
    D. Token ring

4. Which of the following is an advantage of the use of multimedia in the learning process? 4.____

    A. Students can express their abilities in many different ways
    B. It is useful for the students to develop their career in media sciences
    C. It enhances students' motivation for learning
    D. None of the above

5. For the purpose of transfer of technology, companies/organizations must 5.____

    A. allocate much better budget for research and development
    B. have a good networking structure
    C. have willingness to spend on technology to gain long-term benefits
    D. all of the above

6. The focus of teacher education must be on the development of 6.____

    A. professional identity
    B. personal identity
    C. academic identity
    D. none of the above

7. System Study is a study that 7.____

    A. studies an existing system
    B. performs the documentation of the existing system
    C. highlights existing deficiencies and establishes new goals
    D. all of the above

8. Which of these is the starting point for the establishment of an MIS?

   A. Development of physical hardware and networking structure
   B. Development of a DBMS
   C. Understanding and identification of business processes
   D. None of the above

9. A new system is designed by the system analyst by

   A. identifying the subsystems and then creating links among these subsystems
   B. customizing an existing system to the new system
   C. creating a one unit larger system
   D. proposing new system alternatives

10. Process mapping may be defined by which of the following?

    A. Activities are related to the different functional units of the organization
    B. It is developed by the placement of different activities with the help of symbols in a logical order
    A. It is used to present different activities of a process in a hierarchical form
    B. Process efficiency is measured with the help of process mapping

11. Which of the following is an example of a payment system?

    A. E-commerce shopping
    B. Travel reimbursement
    C. Accounts payable
    D. All of the above

12. _____ phase performs problem analysis.

    A. Systems Analysis
    B. System Design
    C. System Implementation
    D. None of the above

13. Top management is most concerned with

    A. daily transactions
    B. strategic decisions
    C. tactical decisions
    D. both (B) and (C)

14. Most companies and organizations have their _____ MIS plans.

    A. master
    B. broad
    C. prototype
    D. control

15. Data integrity refers to

    A. simplicity
    B. security
    C. validity
    D. none of the above

16. The desired outcome for project integration is

    A. better focus on the organization
    B. ideal usage of resources of the organization
    C. better communication among projects and their teams
    D. all of the above

17. If you are working on more than one project and you frequently need to put work on one project on hold and move to another project, then return later to the original project, this is known as

    A. excessive burden
    B. flexible Processing
    C. multitasking
    D. burnout

18. Which of the following may be defined as a project aim?

    A. Meeting the specific quality requirements
    B. On-time delivery
    C. Working within budget constraints
    D. All of the above

19. The progressive phases of management over large projects are best described as

    A. planning, evaluating and scheduling
    B. planning, scheduling and operating
    C. scheduling, planning and operating
    D. planning, scheduling and controlling

20. Variance of the total project completion time is computed in the PERT analysis as

    A. project final activity variance
    B. the aggregation of variances of the project activities
    C. the aggregation of all the activities variance on the critical path
    D. the aggregation of all the activities variance not on the critical path

21. What will be critical path standard deviation if there are three activities -- X, Y and Z -- in the path? X has a deviation of 2, Y has a deviation of 1 and there is a deviation of 2 for Z. In this case, what is the standard deviation of critical path?

    A. 20
    B. 3
    C. 12
    D. 5

22. Linear regression is much similar to

    A. simple moving average forecasting approach
    B. trend project forecasting approach
    C. weighted moving average forecasting approach
    D. naïve forecasting approach

23. The purpose of risk tolerance is to

    A. observe that how much risk can be tolerated by the project
    B. rank project risks
    C. help the project manager in project estimation
    D. help in project scheduling

24. The process group for project management is ordered

    A. initiating, planning, executing, controlling, and closeout
    B. starting, planning, accelerating, and control
    C. planning, establishing, developing, and control
    D. none of the above

25. Which risk management process identifies the workaround?

    A. Risk identification
    B. Risk monitoring
    C. Risk measurement
    D. Risk monitoring and control

KEY (CORRECT ANSWERS)

1. D
2. B
3. C
4. C
5. D

6. A
7. D
8. C
9. A
10. A

11. D
12. A
13. B
14. A
15. C

16. C
17. C
18. D
19. D
20. C

21. B
22. B
23. B
24. A
25. D

TEST 2

DIRECTIONS: Each question or incomplete statement is followed by several suggested answers of completions. Select the one that best answers the question or Complete the statement. *PRINT THE LETTER OF THE CORRECT ANSWER IN THE SPACE AT THE RIGHT.*

1. What is a computer network? 1._____

   A. Information and resource sharing
   B. A combination of computer systems and other hardware elements
   C. A network of communication channels
   D. All of above

2. A network bridge _____. 2.____

   A. monitors network traffic
   B. distinguishes LANs
   C. is a source of connection among LANs
   D. none of the above

3. Which topology is best for the larger networks? 3._____

   A. Ring token
   B. Star
   C. Ring
   D. Bus

4. Interactive books are used in the form of 4._____

   A. educational games
   B. interactive storybooks
   C. interactive texts
   D. both B and C

5. Which of the following are used for GSM technology? 5._____

   A. OFDMA
   B. FDMA/TDMA
   C. CDMA
   D. None of the above

6. What is the main objective of a MIS department? 6._____

   A. To aid the other business areas in performing their tasks
   B. Information processing for the better utilization of data
   C. To be useful for chief executives
   D. To generate useful information

7. Documentation is prepared at 7._____

   A. every phase
   B. the system analysis phase
   C. the system design phase
   D. the system implementation phase

75

8. System prototyping is useful for the

   A. programmer in regards to understanding the whole system
   B. purpose of communication with the users, telling them how the system will look after development
   A. purpose of system demo to the higher project management
   B. Both A and B

9. Mistakes made during the requirements analysis phase normally show up in

   A. system design
   B. system testing
   C. system implementation
   D. none of the above

10. Use case analysis is best described by which of the following statements?

    A. It is used for interface design by highlighting the stages of user interaction with the system
    A. It minimizes the number of steps in order to access the content
    B. A consistent site design with the products and services
    C. It is used for the purpose of information categorization

11. Who is responsible for the analysis and design of the systems?

    A. Developer
    B. System analyst
    C. System operator
    D. Project manager

12. _____ is an outline for the development of bugs-free information systems.

    A. System development life cycle
    B. System conversion
    C. Case tools
    D. System analysis

13. Top-down analysis and design is performed by

    A. the creation of system flow chart after design process
    B. identifying the top-level functions and development of subsequent lower-level components
    C. identifying the root elements and then moving gradually up to the top level
    D. none of the above

14. Which of the following is not the part of marketing mix?

    A. Place
    B. Product
    C. Part
    D. Promotion

15. A distributed MIS mainly deals with the   15._____

    A. local data processing
    B. multiprocessing
    C. sharing of workload
    D. all of the above

16. Project managers unaware of the importance of a project for the organization might tend to   16._____

    A. focus on less important things
    B. emphasize too much on the use of technology
    C. concentrate more on the customer in hand
    D. all of the above

17. Why is it necessary for the project managers to understand the organization's mission?   17._____

    A. To make better decisions and required adjustments
    B. To advocate for projects in a better way
    C. In order to perform their jobs more effectively
    D. Both (A) and (B) are correct

18. Common multi-criteria selection models include   18._____

    A. checklist
    B. NPV
    C. weighted criteria model
    D. both A and C

19. The project management process does not involve   19._____

    A. project scheduling
    B. project planning
    C. system analysis
    D. project estimation

20. Which of the following is the best tool for monitoring projects against the original plan?   20._____

    A. Network diagrams
    B. Gantt Charts
    C. Data Flow diagrams
    D. All of the above

21. A project can be treated as a failed project if   21._____

    A. project requirements are met on schedule
    B. the project is completed on time but with flaws that require additional work
    C. costs are in line with original projections
    D. all of the above

22. Which of the following is a basic assumption of PERT?   22._____

    A. There is no repetition of any activity within the network
    B. There is known time for the completion of each activity
    C. Only the activities in the critical path must be performed
    D. Project start to project end contains only one route

23. Sharing of confidential information with some bidders with the purpose of providing them some undue favor is considered as

    A. bribery
    B. bid rigging
    C. bid fixing
    D. favoritism

24. The advantages of centralized contracting include

    A. provision of easier access to contracting expertise
    B. enhanced organizational contracting expertise
    C. higher level of loyalty
    D. none of the above

25. All of the following are features and characteristics of a project EXCEPT

    A. a defined start and end
    B. a network of related activities
    C. repeated at a regular interval
    D. temporary in nature

KEY (CORRECT ANSWERS)

1. D
2. C
3. B
4. D
5. B

6. A
7. A
8. B
9. C
10. A

11. B
12. A
13. B
14. C
15. C

16. D
17. D
18. D
19. C
20. B

21. B
22. A
23. B
24. B
25. C

TEST 3

DIRECTIONS: Each question or incomplete statement is followed by several suggested answers of completions. Select the one that best answers the question or Complete the statement. *PRINT THE LETTER OF THE CORRECT ANSWER IN THE SPACE AT THE RIGHT.*

1. The number of layers in the OSI Reference Model are

    A. 5
    B. 6
    C. 7
    D. 8

    1.____

2. Which of these is a source of connection oriented message communication?

    A. TCP
    B. UDP
    C. IP
    D. None of the above

    2.____

3. Which buffer is used by the print server for the holding of data before printing?

    A. Node
    B. Spool
    C. Queue
    D. None of above

    3.____

4. Criteria for evaluating commercial hypermedia products include

    A. instructional design
    B. low cost
    C. portability
    D. use of all media channels

    4.____

5. The domain of .net is used by

    A. universities
    B. internet service providers
    C. government organizations
    D. none of the above

    5.____

6. Which of the following is a technology used for the routing of phone calls over a network?

    A. Video-conferencing
    B. VOIP
    C. Teleconferencing
    D. None of the above

    6.____

7. The maintenance phase

    A. defines system requirements
    B. develops system design
    C. performs system testing
    D. none of the above

    7.____

8. Reconstruction of a system requires the consideration of

   A. system inputs and outputs
   B. control and processors
   C. comprehensive user feedback
   D. all of the above

9. Cost-Benefit analysis

   A. performs an estimation of the cost of hardware and software
   B. performs a comparison of costs with the benefits of development of new system
   C. considers both the tangible and non-tangible elements
   D. all of the above

10. Who is responsible for the sponsoring and funding of the project development and its maintenance?

    A. System manager
    B. Project manager
    C. Systems owner
    D. External system user

11. The system implementation approach used in the event you want to run both the old and new systems is called

    A. parallel
    B. pilot
    C. synchronized
    D. phased

12. DBMS advantages include

    A. data integrity
    B. minimization of storage space
    C. centralized access to the data
    D. all of the above

13. Which of the following is a well-known and popular forecasting approach?

    A. Chi Square
    B. Correlation
    C. Regression Analysis
    D. None of the above

14. Who is responsible for the tactical decisions of allocation of resources and establishment of control over project activities?

    A. Middle-level management
    B. Higher-level management
    C. Lower-level management
    D. All of the above

15. The mission statement of an organization answers which of the following questions?

    A. How do we utilize resources?
    B. What are our goals and intentions as an organization?
    C. What are our plans in the long run?
    D. What is the mode of operations in the current environment?

16. What is the benefit of network approach?

    A. Forecasts may be carried on
    B. Structured approach is avoided
    C. Project progress against the original plan can be monitored
    D. Requirement of management judgment is eliminated

17. A Gantt chart is composed of

    A. activities in a sequence
    B. mention of different project activities with the elapsed time
    C. overall project elapsed time
    D. all of the above

18. What does *slack* mean with reference to PERT and CPM?

    A. It is the latest time on which a project may be started without causing any delay for the project
    B. It is a task which must be completed
    C. This reflects the amount of time a specific task may be delayed without having a need to change the overall time of completion of the project
    D. It reflects the start and end time of a task

19. The direct responsibilities of the project manager include

    A. calculation of probability of the task's completion
    B. design of the network diagrams
    C. acting on all aspects of the project
    D. ensuring that all people assigned to a project carry out their required duties and utilize appropriate resources and information in order to perform their tasks

20. What is standard error in a regression forecast?

    A. The highest error level for the forecast
    B. The regression line variability
    C. Time to be consumed for the computation of regression forecast
    D. Forecast validity time

21. Which management process helps in risk identification?

    A. Risk identification, monitoring and control
    B. Qualitative risk analysis
    C. Quantitative risk analysis
    D. Risk detection

22. The cost reimbursable contracts are termed as _____ contracts. 22._____

    A. gradual payment
    B. cost plus
    C. back charge
    D. secure cost

23. The style of conflict resolution that typically has the best impact is 23._____

    A. empathy
    B. problem solving
    C. willingness
    D. mapping

24. Decomposition of deliverables into more manageable components is termed as 24._____

    A. scope segmentation
    B. scope certification
    C. scoping
    D. scope definition

25. What is quality? 25._____

    A. The level at which project requirements are met
    B. Providing output beyond customer demand
    C. Meeting the objectives of management
    D. Meeting customer demands

KEY (CORRECT ANSWERS)

1. C	11. A
2. A	12. D
3. B	13. C
4. A	14. A
5. B	15. B
6. B	16. C
7. D	17. D
8. D	18. C
9. D	19. D
10. C	20. B

21. A
22. B
23. B
24. D
25. A

TEST 4

DIRECTIONS: Each question or incomplete statement is followed by several suggested answers of completions. Select the one that best answers the question or Complete the statement. *PRINT THE LETTER OF THE CORRECT ANSWER IN THE SPACE AT THE RIGHT.*

1. A firewall is a   1._____

   A. tool for web browsing
   B. network boundary established physically
   C. system that blocks unauthorized access
   D. computer's network

2. For data transfer in both directions, which communication approach is utilized?   2._____

   A. Simplex
   B. Half duplex
   C. Full duplex
   D. None of the above

3. Which of the following is utilized for the purpose of modulation and demodulation?   3._____

   A. Satellite
   B. Fiber optics
   C. Modem
   D. Coaxial Cable

4. After looking at the header of the data packet, a _____ decides the destination of the packet.   4._____

   A. hub
   B. switch
   C. router
   D. firewall

5. Which of the following is software for video editing?   5._____

   A. iMovie
   B. ScanImage
   C. PhotoShop
   D. HyperStudio

6. The use of educational technology must be considered as a(n)   6._____

   A. alternative to less technological strategies
   B. necessity for learning
   C. supplement to other teaching tools
   D. none the above

7. Parallel Run refers to   7._____

   A. job processing of two different tasks at two different terminals to compare the outputs
   B. concurrent running of old and new systems in order to identify the likely mistakes of the new system and to perform the daily routine tasks
   C. a job run at two different systems for the purpose of speed comparison
   D. all of the above

8. The purpose of a context diagram is to

   A. establish system context
   B. present the flow of data of the system in order to provide a broader system overview
   C. provide a detailed system description
   D. none of the above

9. The number of steps in the systems development life cycle (SDLC) is

   A. 4
   B. 5
   C. 6
   D. 10

10. Who is the person responsible for ensuring that the project is completed on time with the defined quality and specified budget constraints?

    A. Systems designer
    B. Project manager
    C. Systems owner
    D. Systems manager

11. Which of the following is the deliverable at the system implementation phase?

    A. A solution meeting the specific business needs
    B. Defined business problem
    C. Clear identification of business requirements
    D. A blueprint and sketch of the desired system

12. What type of mail requires proof of delivery?

    A. Express post
    B. External post
    C. Licensed post
    D. Registered post

13. Which of these is a good quality measure?

    A. Authority
    B. Correctness
    C. Precision
    D. All of the above

14. A group of related projects combine to form a _____.

    A. projects classification
    B. product
    C. department
    D. program

15. _____ analysis performs an assessment of internal and external environment.

    A. SWOT
    B. Comprehensive
    C. Organizational
    D. Strategic

16. A dummy activity is required when there is/are

    A. different ending events for more than one activity
    B. one ending event for more than one activity
    C. one starting event for two or more activities
    D. one starting and ending event for more than one activity in the network

17. Limitations of PERT and CPM include

    A. only a limited type of projects can be applied to these
    B. too much consideration is given to the critical path
    C. these are only to monitor the schedules
    D. it is difficult to interpret because of the graphical nature of the network

18. If there is a negative tracking signal against a forecasting, it means

    A. this forecast approach regularly underpredicts
    B. MAPE, too, will be negative
    C. this forecast approach regularly overpredicts
    D. MSE, too, will be negative

19. Quality management is the responsibility of

    A. team Leader
    B. team member
    C. quality assurance coordinator
    D. project manager

20. Purchasing insurance is considered what type of risk?

    A. Recognition
    B. Prevention
    C. Mitigation
    D. Transfer

21. Project costs may be monitored with respect to different categories with the help of

    A. standard accounting practices
    B. chart of accounts
    C. WBS
    D. UAS

22. What is the output of an administrative closure?

    A. Project documentation
    B. Project archives
    C. Risk analysis
    D. None of the above

23. A detailed project budget is created in the _____ process.

    A. establishment
    B. execution
    C. planning
    D. control

24. The person who can gain or lose something from the result of a project activity is the

    A. team member
    B. team leader
    C. supporter
    D. project manager

25. When a project manager apologizes for failing to deal with some issue, this is considered which of the following conflict resolutions?

    A. Forcing
    B. Withdrawal
    C. Compromising
    D. Collaborating

KEY (CORRECT ANSWERS)

1. C
2. C
3. C
4. C
5. A

6. C
7. B
8. B
9. C
10. B

11. A
12. D
13. D
14. D
15. A

16. D
17. B
18. C
19. D
20. D

21. B
22. B
23. C
24. C
25. B

EXAMINATION SECTION
TEST 1

DIRECTIONS: Each question or incomplete statement is followed by several suggested answers or completions. Select the one the BEST answers the question or completes the statement. *PRINT THE LETTER OF THE CORRECT ANSWER IN THE SPACE AT THE RIGHT.*

1. Which of the following was an advantage associated with open source software in the 1990s?　　1.____

    A. A standard user interface for productivity applications such as word processing and spreadsheets
    B. Stringent quality control processes
    C. Suitability for mission-critical applications
    D. A broadened community of programmers who can stabilize and add functionality to software

2. IP addresses　　2.____

    I. are attached to every node on the Internet
    II. are sometimes listed as a character string
    III. establish a direct link between sender and recipient
    IV. use circuit-switching technology

    A. I only
    B. I and II
    C. II, III and IV
    D. I, II, III and IV

3. Programming languages used exclusively for artificial intelligence applications include　　3.____

    A. AIML and Prolog
    B. LISP and Prolog
    C. Ada and LISP
    D. Delphi and Python

4. Cookies are usually stored by browsers as　　4.____

    A. text files
    B. algorithms
    C. tokens
    D. HTML files

5. Analysts typically use each of the following to evaluate the flow of data through an information system, EXCEPT　　5.____

    A. decision trees
    B. Gantt charts
    C. structured English
    D. data flow diagrams

6. Methods for protecting a computer system from viruses include　　6.____

    I. accessing a Web site that offers on-line virus scans

II. checking physical media, such as floppy disks or DVDs, before they are used in a computer
III. erecting a firewall
IV. never opening e-mail attachments from people unknown to the user

A. I and IV
B. II, III and IV
C. III and IV only
D. I, II, III and IV

7. Describing an algorithm as "general" means that it

A. does not have a clear stopping point
B. addresses the stated problem in all instances
C. can be carried out in any sequence
D. can be expressed in any language

8. Packet-switching offers each of the following advantages, EXCEPT

A. faster transmission of data
B. greater network user capacity
C. greater degree of redundancy
D. more localized data corruption

9. The term "digital divide" describes the discrepancies between

A. people who have access to, and the resources to use, new information and communication technologies, and people who do not
B. approximations in the values of floating-point numbers by a processor
C. the rate at which computer processing speeds increase and the rate at which the capacity to store data increases
D. data that is entered into a database application and the information that is displayed to an end-user

10. The main advantage of using programmable microcode is that

A. programs can be made very small and portable
B. the CPU's capacity is never overclocked
C. the same instructions can be executed on different hardware platforms
D. it is usually executed more quickly than other program code

11. Cache memory is NOT

A. used only in large computers
B. used to solve the problem of inadequate primary memory
C. divided into the two main categories of RAM cache and secondary cache
D. used to improve processing speed

12. When PC users ask for a document to be sent to them, they should request a .txt file, because it

A. comes with a built-in antivirus program
B. will only transmit text

C. denotes a disinfected file
D. cannot contain malicious and executable code

13. Line personnel in an organization can enter transaction data and see totals and other results immediately by use of _____ processing

    A. summary
    B. batch
    C. on-line
    D. real-time

14. A network with a main computer that does all of the processing for a number of simple display units is described as

    A. peer-to-peer
    B. client-file server
    C. n-tier
    D. terminal emulation

15. All buses consist of two parts, the _____ bus and the _____ bus.

    A. internal; external
    B. main; expansion
    C. ISA; PCI
    D. address; data

16. The _____ is a small amount of high-speed memory that stores regularly used data.

    A. cache
    B. spool
    C. buffer
    D. frame

17. Technological cornerstones of the Internet include each of the following, EXCEPT

    A. HTML
    B. TCP/IP
    C. URL
    D. MMDS

18. The OSI (Open System Interconnection) model defines a networking framework for implementing protocols in seven layers. The _____ layer, or layer 3, provides switching and routing technologies, creating logical paths, known as virtual circuits, for transmitting data from node to node

    A. network
    B. presentation
    C. transport
    D. session

19. The main difference between the Windows NT operating system and the current Windows OS is that the NT operating system

    A. has no relationship to MS-DOS
    B. has a different user interface
    C. runs faster
    D. supports more peripheral devices

19.____

20. Before sound can be handled on a computer, it must first be converted to electrical energy, and then transformed through an analog-to-digital converter into a digital representation. _____ Law states that the more often a sound wave is sampled, the more accurate the digital representation.

    A. Gilder's
    B. Moore's
    C. Amdahl's
    D. Nyquist's

20.____

21. The primary disadvantage associated with interpreted programming languages, such as Java, is that they

    A. present fewer solutions to individual problems
    B. have slower execution speeds
    C. are not as portable
    D. are more difficult for programmers to understand

21.____

22. The advantages promised by the emerging technology of holographic storage include
    I. higher storage densities
    II. easier synchronization with the CPU
    III. non-volatility
    IV. faster data transfer speeds

    A. I only
    B. I and IV
    C. II and III
    D. III and IV

22.____

23. A file that contains instructions in a particular computer's machine language is said to contain _____ code.

    A. macro
    B. object
    C. scripting
    D. source

23.____

24. A computer uses _____ to transform raw data into useful information.

    A. input devices and output devices
    B. a processor and memory
    C. memory and a motherboard
    D. language and protocols

24.____

25. In computer graphics, the term "raster graphics" is synonymous with

    A. vector graphics
    B. bitmapped graphics
    C. object-oriented graphics
    D. autosizing

26. In 1996, journalist and former White House Press Secretary Pierre Salinger, making a public statement about the causes of the recent TWA Flight 800 crash, became the figurehead for what is now known as the "Pierre Salinger Syndrome" This phenomenon refers to the

    A. act of hiding information by embedding messages within another
    B. pit those who have the skills, knowledge and abilities to use the technologies against those who do not
    C. tendency to believe that everything one reads on the Internet is true
    D. practice of using software to monitor the behavior of a user visiting a Web site or sending an e-mail

27. Which of the following is NOT a term that is interchangeable with "expansion card"?

    A. Expansion file
    B. Expansion board
    C. Adapter
    D. Socket

28. Multidimensional database management systems are also referred to as

    A. Relational database management systems
    B. On-line Transaction Processing (OLTP)
    C. SQL servers
    D. On-line Analytical Processing (OLAP)

29. The primary difference between "smart" and "dumb" printers is that

    A. smart printers can perform dithering
    B. smart printers use a page description language
    C. dumb printers use less system memory
    D. dumb printers cannot bitmap vector graphics

30. The interface between the CPU and the hard disk's electronics is known as the hard disk

    A. navigator
    B. manager
    C. reticulate
    D. controller

31. A single _____ port can be used to connect as many as 127 peripheral devices to a computer.

    A. PIA
    B. Fire Wire
    C. parallel
    D. USB

32. In the binary system, 1011 equals a decimal

    A. 2
    B. 3
    C. 11
    D. 12

33. A transistor radio is an example of _____ transmission of data

    A. half-duplex
    B. full-duplex
    C. half-simplex
    D. simplex

34. Which of the following is NOT a type of liquid crystal display?

    A. Active matrix
    B. Passive matrix
    C. Electroluminescent
    D. Dual-scan

35. Which of the following is a term for commercial software that has been pirated and made available to the public via a bulletin board system (BBS) or the Internet?

    A. Freeware
    B. Crackware
    C. Warez
    D. Shareware

36. IBM-compatible PCs denote the primary hard disk with the

    A. number 1
    B. letter A
    C. letter C
    D. letter X

37. Each of the following operating systems provides some kind of graphical user interface, EXCEPT

    A. Macintosh OS
    B. Linux
    C. UNIX
    D. DOS

38. An operating system's overall quality is most often judged on its ability to manage

    A. program execution
    B. device drivers
    C. disk utilities
    D. application backup

39. In multimedia product development, elements of a program are arranged into separate

    A. tracks
    B. columns

C. zones
D. layers

40. The CPU contains the _____ unit.
    I. I/O
    II. control
    III. arithmetic
    IV. instructing decoding

    A. I and II
    B. I, II and IV
    C. II and V
    D. I, II, III and IV

41. The on-line application that locates and displays the document associated with a hyper-link is a(n)

    A. server
    B. plug-in
    C. browser
    D. finder

42. Which of the following devices requires a driver?
    I. printer
    II. mouse
    III. DVD drive
    IV. keyboard

    A. I only
    B. I, II and IV
    C. II and IV
    D. I, II, III and IV

43. Database management systems include each of the following components, EXCEPT

    A. data collection applications
    B. statistical analysis applications
    C. data modification applications
    D. query languages

44. Waves are characterized by each of the following, EXCEPT

    A. Frequency
    B. Pulse
    C. Frequency
    D. Amplitude

45. Although considered to be outdated by many programmers, _____ is still the most widely used programming language in the world.

    A. Pascal
    B. COBOL
    C. FORTRAN
    D. BASIC

46. A graphics program using the _____ model represents three-dimensional objects by displaying their outlines and edges.

    A. wireframe
    B. volumetric
    C. solid
    D. surface

47. The concept central to the legislation that regulates telephone service in the United States is

    A. broadband service
    B. consumer price parity
    C. reasonable access time
    D. universal access

48. In order to be certified as "open source" by the Open Source Institute (OSI), a program must meet each of the following criteria, EXCEPT that the

    A. rights attached to the program are contingent on the program's being part of a particular software distribution
    B. author or holder of the license of the source code cannot collect royalties on the distribution of the program
    C. distributed program must make the source code accessible to the user
    D. licensed software cannot place restrictions on other software distributed with it

49. Ethernet systems typically use a _____ topology.

    A. bus
    B. star
    C. ring
    D. tree

50. In enterprises, the _____ is the computer that routes the traffic from a workstation to the outside network that is serving the Web pages.

    A. proxy server
    B. ISP
    C. packet switcher
    D. gateway

KEY (CORRECT ANSWERS)

1. D	11. A	21. B	31. D	41. C
2. B	12. D	22. B	32. C	42. D
3. B	13. C	23. B	33. D	43. A
4. A	14. A	24. B	34. C	44. B
5. B	15. D	25. B	35. C	45. B
6. D	16. A	26. C	36. C	46. A
7. B	17. D	27. D	37. D	47. D
8. A	18. A	28. D	38. A	48. A
9. A	19. A	29. B	39. A	49. A
10. C	20. D	30. D	40. B	50. D

TEST 2

DIRECTIONS: Each question or incomplete statement is followed by several suggested answers or completions. Select the one the BEST answers the question or completes the statement. *PRINT THE LETTER OF THE CORRECT ANSWER IN THE SPACE AT THE RIGHT.*

1. "Refresh rate" typically refers to the

    A. number of times RAM is updated in a second
    B. time it takes to completely rewrite a disk
    C. number of times the display monitor is redrawn in a second
    D. time it takes for a Web pages to reload

    1.____

2. In a markup language, authors use _____ to identify portions of a document.

    A. icons
    B. schemas
    C. numbers
    D. elements

    2.____

3. Object-oriented programming languages rely heavily on _____ to create high-level objects.
    - I. formalization
    - II. abstraction
    - III. information hiding
    - IV. encapsulation

    A. I only
    B. I, II and III
    C. II, III and IV
    D. I, II, III and IV

    3.____

4. The base unit of three-dimensional graphics is the

    A. texel
    B. voxel
    C. pixel
    D. bit

    4.____

5. In computing, "gamma correction" typically refers to an adjustment in the

    A. light intensity of a scanner, monitor, or printer
    B. amplitude modulation
    C. emission of gamma waves by a CRT monitor
    D. speed with which analog data is digitized

    5.____

6. The OSI (Open System Interconnection) model defines a networking framework for implementing protocols in seven layers. The seventh layer of the OSI model consists of the

    A. hardware
    B. applications

    6.____

C. protocols
D. network

7. A significant difference between frame switching packet switching is that frame switching

    A. offers accelerated packet processing
    B. creates a virtual circuit
    C. allows multiple connections on the same set of hardware
    D. contains now quality-of-service assurances

7.____

8. In _____ memory, each location has an actual "address."

    A. RAM
    B. ROM
    C. PROM
    D. EPROM

8.____

9. Video applications require a bare minimum of _____ frames per second in order to function.

    A. 8
    B. 15
    C. 30
    D. 60

9.____

10. The most commonly used network application today is

    A. Web design
    B. BBS
    C. e-mail
    D. software downloading

10.____

11. Standardized codes for representing character data numerically include
        I. ANSI
        II. EBCDIC
        III. ASCII
        IV. DECS

    A. I and II
    B. II and III
    C. II, III and IV
    D. I, II, III and IV

11.____

12. Photolithography is the process of transferring geometric shapes on a mask to the surface of a silicon wafer. Possible future alternative technologies to photolithography include each of the following, EXCEPT the

    A. multiple-wave laser beam
    B. electron beam
    C. extreme ultraviolet
    D. X-ray

12.____

13. Hard disk mechanisms typically contain a single

    A. head actuator
    B. read/write head
    C. platter
    D. landing zone

14. Contemporary Rapid Application Development (RAD) emphasizes the reduction of development time through

    A. trimming code
    B. inserting pre-written artificial intelligence capabilities
    C. establishing a graphical user interface
    D. making slight modifications to proprietary software

15. A Web site contains a number of databases that contain all the information about an organization's clients-such as names, addresses, credit card information, past invoices, etc.). This is an example of a data

    A. mine
    B. warehouse
    C. dictionary
    D. mart

16. Currently, a computer's most difficult task would be to

    A. speak in long paragraphs
    B. recognize spoken words
    C. interpret the meaning of words
    D. compose a syntactically correct item of discourse

17. An API is a(n)

    A. algorithm for the lossless compression of files
    B. set of routines, protocols, and tools for building software applications
    C. piece of software that helps the operating system communicate with a peripheral device
    D. code for representing characters as numbers

18. The disadvantages associated with ring LAN topologies include
    I. more limited geographical range
    II. low bandwidth
    III. high expense
    IV. complex and difficult installation

    A. I only
    B. I and II
    C. III and IV
    D. I, II, III and IV

19. Scientists would most likely use _____ to analyze variations in planetary orbits.

    A. a mainframe
    B. the Internet

C. a supercomputer
D. a virtual network

20. The primary disadvantage to shared-memory multiprocessing involves 20.____

   A. slow retrieval speeds
   B. bus overload
   C. inadequate trace width
   D. RAM purges

21. If a computer user enters a legal command that does not make any sense in the given 21.____
    context, the user has committed an error of

   A. syntax
   B. semantics
   C. formatting
   D. parsing

22. Which of the following terms is NOT synonymous with the others? 22.____

   A. Floating point unit
   B. Numeric coprocessor
   C. Math coprocessor
   D. Accelerator board

23. Which of the following is a measure of data transfer capacity? 23.____

   A. Duplication rate
   B. Bandwidth
   C. Frequency
   D. Baud rate

24. In the 1990s, the main obstacle to the use of the Linux operating system in desktop appli- 24.____
    cations was

   A. the lack of a standard user interface
   B. difficulties in file and print serving
   C. inability to accommodate multiple platforms
   D. insufficient support from the commercial sector

25. Which of the following external bus standards supports "hot plugging"–the ability to add 25.____
    and remove devices to a computer while the computer is running and have the operating
    system automatically recognize the change?

   A. Serial
   B. USB
   C. PCI
   D. Parallel port

26. When a key on a computer keyboard is struck, each of the following may occur, EXCEPT 26.____

   A. a cursor on the screen moves
   B. a scan code is sent to an application

C. a binary number is input into the computer
D. an EBCDIC code for a letter is sent to a word processing application

27. SONET

    A. cannot be used to link digital networks to fiber optics
    B. is a synchronous Layer 1 protocol
    C. prohibits data streams of different speeds from being multiplexed in the same line
    D. can scale up to 4 Gbps

28. A user handles data stored on a disk with the utility program known as the

    A. file sorter
    B. file manager
    C. disk scanner
    D. finder

29. A _____ is a tool that helps users of word processing or desktop publishing applications to avoid formatting complex documents individually.

    A. merge
    B. column
    C. template
    D. table

30. Which of the following is a high-level programming language that is particularly suited for use on the World Wide Web, often through the use of small, downloadable applications known as applets?

    A. XML
    B. Ada
    C. Java
    D. C++

31. Microprocessor speeds have increased dramatically over the past two decades, largely as a result of significant

    A. improvements in hardware breakpoints
    B. increases in trace depth
    C. compression of overlay RAM
    D. reductions in trace width

32. On most PCs, this contains all the code required to control the keyboard, display screen, disk drives, serial communications, and a number of miscellaneous functions.

    A. Flash memory
    B. Operating system
    C. BIOS
    D. USB

33. Which of the following is a rating system originally designed to help parents and teachers control what children access on the Internet, but now also used to facilitate other uses for labels, including code signing and privacy?

    A. V-chip
    B. Recreational Software Advisory Council
    C. Platform for Internet Content Selection
    D. Cyber Patrol

33.____

34. A database designed for continuous addition and deletion of records is said to perform the function of _____ processing.

    A. batch
    B. drilldown
    C. transaction
    D. analytical

34.____

35. A unique 128-bit number, produced by the Windows OS or by some Windows applications to identify a particular component, application, file, database entry, and/or user is known as a

    A. key
    B. GUID
    C. PGP
    D. DLL

35.____

36. Compared to private-key cryptograph, public-key

    A. uses two keys
    B. is easier to understand
    C. functions more smoothly with contemporary networks
    D. requires fewer computations

36.____

37. Static RAM (SRAM) is used to

    A. supplement the main memory
    B. determine which information should be kept in the cache
    C. form the memory cache
    D. form the disk cache

37.____

38. A(n) _____ system is used to produce reports that will help managers throughout an organization to evaluate their departments.

    A. expert
    B. management information
    C. office automation
    D. transaction processing

38.____

39. Software that may be delivered/downloaded and used without charge, but is nevertheless still copyrighted by the author, is known as

    A. public-domain software
    B. shareware

39.____

C. open-source software
D. freeware

40. Barriers to widespread use of cable modems in Internet access include
    I. the one-way transmission design of the television infrastructure
    II. uncertain capacity of television infrastructure
    III. complexity of protocols
    IV. bandwidth restrictions

    A. I only
    B. I and II
    C. II and IV
    D. I, II, III and IV

41. Which of the following is NOT a function that can be performed with a spreadsheet application?

    A. Budget charts and graphs
    B. Inventory management
    C. Audiovisual presentations
    D. Fiscal forecasting

42. Which of the following is a Windows-based graphical user interface for the UNIX operating system?

    A. Linux
    B. Gnu
    C. MOTIF
    D. UNI

43. In a database, the _____ contains a code, number, name, or some other information that uniquely identifies the record.

    A. primary key
    B. file
    C. schema
    D. key field

44. Which of the following terms is NOT synonymous with the others?

    A. Web bug
    B. Clear GIF
    C. Web beacon
    D. Cookie

45. As a firewall technology, the proxy server operates by

    A. examining each packet that enters or exits a network, and accepts or rejects it based on a given set of rules
    B. applying security mechanisms to specific applications
    C. constantly changing its location
    D. intercepting all messages entering and leaving a network

46. VRAM is a specific kind of memory used to

    A. accelerate processing speeds
    B. store video display data
    C. create virtual addresses, rather than real addresses, to store data and instructions
    D. create a virtual environment for the user

47. Which phase of the application development process serves to identify features that must be added to the program to make it satisfactory to users?

    A. Software concept
    B. Coding and debugging
    C. System testing
    D. Requirements analysis

48. What is the term for the natural data size of a computer?

    A. Word size
    B. Clock speed
    C. Bus width
    D. Cache

49. Microkernels operate by moving many of the operating system services into "user space" that other operating systems keep in the kernel. This migration tends to have each of the following effects, EXCEPT greater

    A. security
    B. bug immunity for the kernel
    C. configurability
    D. "fixed" memory footprint

50. High-level programming languages are
    I. useful when speed is essential
    II. processor-independent
    III. usually compiled or assembled
    IV. easier to read, write and maintain than other languages

    A. I and IV
    B. I, II, and III
    C. II, III and IV
    D. I, II, III and IV

KEY (CORRECT ANSWERS)

1. C	11. C	21. B	31. D	41. C
2. D	12. A	22. D	32. C	42. C
3. C	13. A	23. B	33. C	43. A
4. A	14. C	24. A	34. C	44. D
5. A	15. B	25. B	35. B	45. D
6. B	16. C	26. D	36. A	46. B
7. B	17. B	27. B	37. C	47. C
8. A	18. C	28. B	38. B	48. A
9. B	19. C	29. C	39. C	49. D
10. C	20. B	30. C	40. B	50. C

EXAMINATION SECTION
TEST 1

DIRECTIONS: Each question or incomplete statement is followed by several suggested answers or completions. Select the one the BEST answers the question or completes the statement. *PRINT THE LETTER OF THE CORRECT ANSWER IN THE SPACE AT THE RIGHT.*

1. Which of the following types of firewall techniques is most susceptible to IP spoofing? 1.____

    A. Proxy server
    B. Circuit-level gateway
    C. Packet filter
    D. Application gateway

2. Which of the following is a term for unorganized symbols, words, images, numbers or sound that a computer can transform into something useful? 2.____

    A. Software
    B. Data
    C. Input
    D. Information

3. In relational databases, records are referred to as 3.____

    A. stories
    B. tuples
    C. keys
    D. files

4. Web _____ can be included in HTML-formatted e-mail messages to reveal whether a recipient has received a message, as well as to disclose the recipient's IP address. 4.____

    A. cookies
    B. bots
    C. bugs
    D. tokens

5. Which of the following is NOT typically an element of a GUI? 5.____

    A. Column
    B. Icon
    C. Pointer
    D. Menu

6. Of the three general methods for posing queries to a database, choosing parameters from a menu 6.____

    A. is the least flexible
    B. is the most powerful
    C. requires the user to learn a specialized language
    D. presents the user with a blank record and lets him/her specify fields and values

7. Unless the circuitry is part of a workstation's design, LAN computers usually need a(n) _____ to function in the network.   7.____

   A. NIC
   B. bus
   C. protocol
   D. EDI

8. A VPN enables a business to   8.____

   A. avoid network "tear-downs"
   B. make use of the Internet, rather than build a dedicated network
   C. make a network inherently more secure
   D. work on circuits, rather than packets

9. In a client/server architecture, the component that performs the bulk of the data processing operations is known as the   9.____

   A. fat client
   B. portal
   C. server
   D. node

10. The process of translating virtual addresses into real addresses is known as   10.____

    A. paging
    B. ghosting
    C. mapping
    D. swapping

11. The first commercially developed operating system was   11.____

    A. OS1
    B. Windows
    C. OS360
    D. DOS

12. The relationships between cells in a spreadsheet application are known as   12.____

    A. formulas
    B. references
    C. attributes
    D. labels

13. Most contemporary personal computers come with external cache memory that sits between the CPU and the main memory. This cache is known as the _____ cache.   13.____

    A. disk
    B. DRAM
    C. Level 1 (L1)
    D. Level 2 (L2)

14. Only _____ language programs can manipulate CPU registers.
    I. machine
    II. assembly
    III. high-level
    IV. fourth-generation

    A. I and II
    B. II only
    C. I, II and III
    D. IV only

15. In the _____ process, the amplitude of an analog wave is checked at regular intervals in order to enable its encoding into digital form.

    A. attenuation
    B. sampling
    C. amplification
    D. modulation

16. In the _____ phase of the systems development life cycle, programmers either write software from scratch or purchase software from a vendor.

    A. implementation
    B. maintenance
    C. needs analysis
    D. development

17. The term "warm boot" refers to

    A. getting a quick view of stored files
    B. placing files in a more secure location
    C. restarting a computer that is already on
    D. making files more quickly available on a disk

18. In terms of digital security, nonrepudiation can be accomplished through each of the following, EXCEPT

    A. confirmation services
    B. timestamps
    C. nym servers
    D. digital signatures

19. More advanced microprocessors may begin executing a second instruction before the first has been complete. This is a feature known as

    A. multitasking
    B. burst mode
    C. pipelining
    D. cascading

20. The main disadvantage associated with ATM network technology is that it   20.____

    A. tends to favor audio and video over traditional data
    B. creates cells of unpredictable size
    C. does not respond well to fluctuations in network traffic
    D. requires large startup costs

21. Computer users make use of hypertext in browser software by clicking the mouse on a   21.____

    A. graphic image
    B. pull-down menu choice
    C. hot spot
    D. button

22. Products using the IEEE 1394 interface may use each of the following names, EXCEPT   22.____

    A. i.link
    B. USB
    C. Fire Wire
    D. Lynx

23. What is the term for the computer's processing circuitry, located within the system's case?   23.____

    A. CPU
    B. RAM
    C. Motherboard
    D. BIOS

24. The primary difficulty in using a LAN to directly connect telephone calls to a server is that   24.____

    A. it would prevent the LAN from working with another remote network
    B. the configuration of the network would change into something that could not strictly be considered a "LAN"
    C. most LAN technologies don't handle voice data very well
    D. the link would require synchronous data

25. Graphical software developers can create virtual environments from two-dimensional images by making use of   25.____

    A. Quicktime VR
    B. MPEG
    C. transcoding
    D. Cinepak

26. In the design of an information system, a(n) _____ is often useful to show all organizations, departments, users, applications, and data that function in the system.   26.____

    A. Gantt chart
    B. data dictionary
    C. schema
    D. entity-relationship diagram

27. Which of the following terms is NOT synonymous with the others? 27.____

    A. Bit rate
    B. Vertical frequency
    C. Refresh rate
    D. Frame rate

28. What is the term for the process of adding depth to an image using a volumetric dataset (a set of cross-sectional images)? 28.____

    A. Voxelization
    B. Texelization
    C. Interpixellation
    D. Rounding out

29. Assembly language must be translated into _____ before it can run on a computer. 29.____

    A. source code
    B. pseudocode
    C. machine language
    D. BASIC

30. Indexing a database field offers the benefit of 30.____

    A. establishing an encryption code for selected data items
    B. allowing for the programming of an interface
    C. duplicating information contained within the field for backup purposes
    D. accelerating searches in that field

31. Some computer keyboards have a(n) _____ integrated into them, between the g and h keys. 31.____

    A. mini-mouse
    B. trackball
    C. light pen
    D. integrated pointing device

32. Which of the following is a 16-bit standard for denoting characters that can represent most of the world's languages? 32.____

    A. ANSI
    B. ASCII
    C. Unicode
    D. ISO Latin-1

33. Mosaic is a _____ browser. 33.____

    A. graphical
    B. text-only
    C. markup
    D. plug-in

34. Which of the following can be used to enhance the performance of executing commands on a database?

    A. Connection pools
    B. Two-phase commits
    C. Fixed lengths
    D. Triggers

35. The FIRST step in the photolithographic process is

    A. soft baking
    B. wafer cleaning
    C. barrier layer formation
    D. mask alignment

36. Computer program instructions
    I. are explicit and unequivocal
    II. perform only one task each
    III. are translated into binary code before execution
    IV. are executed in sequence

    A. I and II
    B. I, II and III
    C. III and IV
    D. I, II, III and IV

37. When transferred to a different computer, a(n) _____ language requires very little reprogramming.

    A. high-level
    B. machine
    C. assembly
    D. natural

38. Typically, the operating system kernel is responsible for managing each of the following, EXCEPT

    A. peripherals
    B. program execution
    C. memory
    D. disk

39. The UNIX operating system was the first major program written in the computer language

    A. Ada
    B. C
    C. Java
    D. C++

40. The _____ version of a software product is given to manufacturers to bundle into future versions of their hardware products. 40._____

    A. alpha
    B. maintenance
    C. crippled
    D. RTM

41. MOUS is an acronym that stands for 41._____

    A. Memory Overload/Unusable System
    B. Modulation User Set
    C. Microsoft Office Utility Service
    D. Microsoft Office User Specialist

42. The opposite of "time sharing" in microprocessing is 42._____

    A. multitasking
    B. autosizing
    C. multiprocessing
    D. batch processing

43. A standard compact disc can contain about _____ MB of data. 43._____

    A. 480
    B. 650
    C. 720
    D. 800

44. Which of the following is LEAST similar to the others in its function? 44._____

    A. Extension
    B. Command file
    C. Script
    D. Macro

45. Tools for analyzing data in spreadsheet programs include each of the following, EXCEPT 45._____

    A. conceptual problem-solving
    B. risk modeling
    C. sensitivity analysis
    D. goal seeking

46. Many optical scanners are capable of gray scaling, and typically use from _____ different shades of gray. 46._____

    A. 8 to 32
    B. 16 to 256
    C. 512 to 1024
    D. 300 to 600

47. A language that is designed to specify the layout of a document is known as a(n) _____ language.

   A. object-oriented
   B. query
   C. assembly
   D. markup

48. A hacker enters the computer system of his credit card company and changes a charge from $1,250.00 to $12.50. This is an example of the computer crime known as

   A. Van Eck bugging
   B. salami attack
   C. piggybacking
   D. data diddling

49. In the hexadecimal coding system, 1111 equals the

   A. number two
   B. number four
   C. letter D
   D. letter F

50. A URL may include information about
   I. what protocol to use
   II. the IP address
   III. the domain name
   IV. the type of file

   A. I and II
   B. II and III
   C. II, III and IV
   D. I, II, III and IV

KEY (CORRECT ANSWERS)

1. C	11. C	21. D	31. D	41. D
2. B	12. A	22. B	32. C	42. D
3. B	13. D	23. A	33. C	43. B
4. C	14. B	24. C	34. A	44. A
5. A	15. B	25. A	35. B	45. A
6. A	16. D	26. D	36. D	46. B
7. A	17. C	27. A	37. A	47. D
8. B	18. C	28. A	38. A	48. D
9. A	19. C	29. C	39. B	49. D
10. C	20. C	30. D	40. D	50. D

TEST 2

DIRECTIONS: Each question or incomplete statement is followed by several suggested answers or completions. Select the one the BEST answers the question or completes the statement. *PRINT THE LETTER OF THE CORRECT ANSWER IN THE SPACE AT THE RIGHT.*

1. Because of their vertical arrangement, the OSI Reference Model and the TCP/IP protocols are referred to as network protocol   1.____

    A. towers
    B. stacks
    C. dunes
    D. compilers

2. _____ of the operating system are less frequently used, and copied from the disk as needed.   2.____

    A. Nonresident
    B. Peripheral
    C. Application
    D. Unthreaded

3. Presentation programs such as PowerPoint often use the _____ effect to blend slides together while switching from one to the next.   3.____

    A. dithering
    B. transition
    C. slumping
    D. fade-in

4. In a network in which transactions are being recorded, the _____ strategy is designed to ensure that either all the databases on the network are updated or none of them, so that the databases remain synchronized.   4.____

    A. dynaset
    B. two-phase commit
    C. failover
    D. aggregate function

5. Which of the following is an optical storage device?   5.____

    A. CD-ROM
    B. Floppy disk
    C. Hard disk
    D. Cassette tape

6. The capacity of RAM is measured in   6.____

    A. bytes
    B. kilobytes
    C. megabytes
    D. gigabytes

7. The four stages of the CPU's operation cycle, in sequence, are

    A. execute, store, decode, fetch
    B. fetch, execute, translate, store
    C. fetch, decode, execute, store
    D. encode, store, decode, fetch

8. In a database application, a _____ check validation would ensure that a worker's salary did not exceed the maximum of $53,599.

    A. range
    B. completeness
    C. sequence
    D. consistency

9. In a _____ network, all nodes have equivalent capabilities and responsibilities.

    A. peer-to-peer
    B. file server
    C. frame relay
    D. client/server

10. Which of the following is NOT a common technology for the storage of binary information?

    A. Analog
    B. Magnetic
    C. Optical
    D. Electronic

11. Typically, the term "legacy application" is applied to

    A. productivity software
    B. newer, more innovative programs
    C. database management systems
    D. operating systems

12. Which of the following is NOT an example of a database application?

    A. Parts inventory system
    B. Automated teller machine
    C. Mortgage calculator
    D. Flight reservations system

13. A computer component may signal the CPU that it has data available by

    A. shorting the bus
    B. fetching an instruction
    C. flushing the pipeline
    D. sending an interrupt

14. The hexadecimal numbering system uses a base of 14.____

    A. eight
    B. twelve
    C. sixteen
    D. thirty-two

15. POSIX is 15.____

    A. a set of standards to make applications independent of the UNIX operating system
    B. an open-source alternative to the UNIX operating system
    C. a set of standards that makes an operating system look like UNIX to an application
    D. a specialized form of the UNIX operating system for use in medical/ health care applications

16. The type of programming language that most closely mirrors human ways of thinking is _____ language. 16.____

    A. assembly
    B. object-oriented
    C. translator
    D. query

17. The main reason hard disks are used to store data instead of much faster technologies, such as DRAM, is because hard disks are 17.____

    A. capable of reorganizing data from location to location
    B. less prone to read/write errors
    C. more amenable to recovery if something goes wrong
    D. not volatile

18. The final step in producing an executable program is to 18.____

    A. translate pseudocode into source code
    B. translate the source code into object code
    C. translate source code into a language such as C or FORTRAN
    D. transform the object code into machine language

19. What is the term for software that has been written into ROM? 19.____

    A. Warez
    B. Pseudocode
    C. Firmware
    D. Macrocode

20. Variables play an important role in computer programming because they enable programmers to 20.____

    A. maintain strict quality-control standards
    B. make programs backward compatible
    C. avoid repeated iterations
    D. write flexible programs

21. The foremost organization for information systems personnel and managers is the

    A. Data Processing Management Association
    B. United States Chief Information Officers Council
    C. Information Resources Management Association
    D. Association of Internet Professionals

22. Second-generation graphics systems improved upon first-generation systems by

    A. adding shading capabilities
    B. supporting texture-mapping
    C. allowing for the movement of objects in 3D space
    D. enabling full-scene antialiasing

23. Suitable standards for testing the quality of a computer program include each of the following, EXCEPT

    A. semantic errors
    B. logic errors
    C. robustness
    D. reliability

24. Bitmap file formats include each of the following, EXCEPT

    A. GIF
    B. CGM
    C. PNG
    D. DIB

25. The largest collection of information in a database is the

    A. file
    B. system
    C. field
    D. record

26. Of the telephone technologies listed below, the oldest is

    A. FDDI
    B. PSTN
    C. SONET
    D. ISDN

27. The primary difference between a "workstation" and a regular desktop system lies in

    A. graphics capabilities
    B. the operating system
    C. microprocessing speeds
    D. the number of users

28. In contemporary personal computers, the stripped-down operating system is stored in _____ before a computer is turned on.

    A. RAM
    B. ROM
    C. the hard disk
    D. the CPU

29. When a computer is multitasking, the _____ controls the flow of program tasks through the CPU.

    A. RAM
    B. CPU
    C. disk cache
    D. operating system

30. A digital pulse, viewed on an oscilloscope, appears as a

    A. square wave
    B. short dash
    C. microwave
    D. gamma wave

31. The first operating system developed with preemptive multitasking was

    A. MS-DOS
    B. OS/2
    C. Windows
    D. UNIX

32. Each of the following methods of data compression may involve temporal compression, EXCEPT

    A. JPEG
    B. Content-based
    C. MPEG
    D. P-frame

33. A network manager is considering the implementation of ATM technology. Because the organization uses the network primarily for file transfers, the most appropriate type of ATM service would be _____ bit rate.

    A. available
    B. variable
    C. constant
    D. unspecified

34. Which type of color model is typically used in commercial printing?

    A. CIE
    B. RGB
    C. HGB
    D. CMYK

35. The _____ is an allotted space in which spreadsheet programs allow users to create and edit data and formulas.

   A. register
   B. formula bar
   C. data field
   D. status bar

36. The four-layered protocol that was instrumental in the expansion of the Internet is

   A. OSI
   B. ATM
   C. TCP/IP
   D. UDP/IP

37. The most common top-level domain name suffix used on the World Wide Web is

   A. .gov
   B. .edu
   C. .org
   D. .com

38. The process of synchronizing databases that exist in different localities is known as

   A. replication
   B. distribution
   C. storehousing
   D. backup

39. Productivity software that uses a document-centric approach is made possible by the compound document standards known as

   A. XML and HTML
   B. VAP and AWT
   C. JFS and ISAM
   D. OLE and OpenDoc

40. What is the term for a WAN or LAN that uses TCP/IP protocols and can be accessed only by users from within the organization that owns the network?

   A. Extranet
   B. Intranet
   C. Supranet
   D. Isonet

41. File compression technologies that attempt to eliminate redundant or unnecessary information, such as the technology used with MPEG files, are described as

   A. terse
   B. DCT
   C. lossy
   D. stripped

42. What is the term for a database that is designed to help managers make strategic business decisions?

    A. Data mine
    B. Operational data store
    C. Data mart
    D. Data warehouse

    42._____

43. Which type of computer virus exploits the automatic command execution capabilities of certain types of application software?

    A. Macro virus
    B. Worm
    C. Trojan horse
    D. Zombie

    43._____

44. All computers use a _____ to translate between digital code and audio signals.

    A. sound card
    B. SMDI
    C. audio scrubber
    D. Sound Blaster

    44._____

45. A hard disk's storage capacity can be increased by means of

    A. caching
    B. virtual memory
    C. boot blocking
    D. file compression

    45._____

46. _____ a standard for describing the location of resources on the World Wide Web.

    A. FTP
    B. URL
    C. XML
    D. HTML

    46._____

47. Which of the following is a multithreading operating system?

    A. UNIX
    B. MS-DOS
    C. VMS
    D. Linux

    47._____

48. Probably the easiest method for committing computer crime today is

    A. shoulder surfing
    B. piggybacking
    C. Trojan horses
    D. below-threshold attacks

    48._____

49. Which of the following types of servers enables users to log on to a host computer and perform tasks as if they're working on the remote computer itself? 49.____

   A. Middleware
   B. Telnet
   C. IRC
   D. FTP

50. _____ occurs when a programmer places source code and a compiler or interpreter on a different computer platform, and then creates working object code. 50.____

   A. Assembling
   B. Reconfiguring
   C. Replication
   D. Porting

KEY (CORRECT ANSWERS)

1. B	11. C	21. A	31. D	41. C
2. A	12. C	22. A	32. A	42. C
3. B	13. D	23. A	33. D	43. A
4. B	14. C	24. B	34. D	44. A
5. A	15. C	25. A	35. B	45. D
6. A	16. B	26. B	36. C	46. B
7. C	17. D	27. A	37. D	47. D
8. A	18. D	28. B	38. A	48. A
9. A	19. C	29. D	39. D	49. B
10. A	20. D	30. A	40. B	50. D

EXAMINATION SECTION
TEST 1

DIRECTIONS: Each question or incomplete statement is followed by several suggested answers or completions. Select the one that BEST answers the question or completes the statement. *PRINT THE LETTER OF THE CORRECT ANSWER IN THE SPACE AT THE RIGHT.*

1. Representations of human knowledge used in expert systems generally include each of the following EXCEPT

    A. frames
    B. semantic nets
    C. fuzzy logic
    D. rules

2. Routines performed to verify input data and correct errors prior to processing are known as

    A. edit checks
    B. pilots
    C. control aids
    D. data audits

3. Which of the following statements about database management systems is generally FALSE?
They

    A. are able to separate logical and physical views of data
    B. eliminate data confusion by providing central control of data creation and definitions
    C. reduce data redundancy
    D. involve slight increases in program development and maintenance costs

4. In systems theory, there is a *what-if* method of treating uncertainty that explores the effect on the alternatives of environmental change. This method is generally referred to as _____ analysis.

    A. sensitivity
    B. contingency
    C. a fortiori
    D. systems

5. One of the core capabilities of a decision support system (DSS) is the logical and mathematical manipulation of data_____ a capability referred to as

    A. control aids
    B. representations
    C. memory aids
    D. operations

6. What is the term for the ability to move software from one generation of hardware to another more powerful generation?

    A. Adaptability
    B. Interoperability
    C. Multitasking
    D. Migration

7. In an enterprise information system, which of the following is considered to be an input control?

    A. Documentation of operating procedures
    B. Reviews of processing logs
    C. Verification of control totals
    D. Program testing

121

8. Low-speed transmission of data that occurs one character at a time is described as   8._____

   A. asynchronous B. unchained
   C. phased   D. unstructured

9. Which of the following is a disadvantage associated with the use of relational databases?   9._____

   A. Limited ability to combine information from different sources
   B. Simplicity in maintenance
   C. Relatively slower speed of operation
   D. Limited flexibility regarding ad hoc queries

10. When all the elements in a system are in the same category, _____ is said to be at a minimum.   10._____

    A. uncertainty   B. synergy
    C. inefficiency D. entropy

11. Which of the following is most likely to rely on parallel processing?   11._____

    A. Minicomputer   B. Workstation
    C. Microcomputer D. Supercomputer

12. In imaging systems, what is the term for the device that allows a user to identify and retrieve a specific document?   12._____

    A. Forward chain   B. Index server
    C. Knowledge base D. Search engine

13. Which of the following systems exists at the strategic level of an organization?   13._____

    A. Decision support system (DSS)
    B. Executive support system (ESS)
    C. Knowledge work system (KWS)
    D. Management information system (MIS)

14. What is the term for the secondary storage device on which a complete operating system is stored?   14._____

    A. Central Processing Unit   B. Microprocessor
    C. Optical code recognizer   D. System residence drive

15. Which of the following is NOT a type of knowledge work system (KWS)?   15._____

    A. Investment workstations
    B. Virtual reality systems
    C. Computer-aided design (CAD)
    D. Decision support system (DSS)

16. A transmission over a telecommunications network in which data can flow two ways, but in only one direction at a time, is described as   16._____

    A. simplex   B. half duplex
    C. full duplex D. multiplex

17. The functions of knowledge workers in an organization generally include each of the following EXCEPT

    A. updating knowledge
    B. managing documentation of knowledge
    C. serving as internal consultants
    D. acting as change agents

18. The predominant programming language for business was

    A. Perl   B. COBOL   C. FORTRAN   D. SGML

19. In general, the technology associated with reduced instruction set (RISC) computers is most appropriate for

    A. decision support systems (DSS)
    B. network communications
    C. scientific and workstation computing
    D. desktop publishing

20. Which of the following signifies the international reference model for linking different types of computers and networks?

    A. WAN   B. ISDN   C. TCP/IP   D. OSI

21. The main difference between neural networks and expert systems is that neural networks

    A. seek a generalized capability to learn
    B. program solutions
    C. are aimed at solving one specific problem at a time
    D. seek to emulate or model a person's way of solving a set of problems

22. Which of the following is not a management benefit associated with end-user development of information systems?

    A. Reduced application backlog
    B. Increased user satisfaction
    C. Simplified testing and documentation procedures
    D. Improved requirements determination

23. Which of the following is NOT an example of an output control associated with information systems?

    A. Balancing output totals with input and processing totals
    B. formal procedures and documentation specifying recipients of reports and checks
    C. Error handling
    D. Review of computer processing logs

24. Of the following statements about the evolutionary planning method of strategic information systems design, which is FALSE?
    It is

    A. a top-down method
    B. high adaptive
    C. best for use in a dynamic environment
    D. susceptible to domination by a few users

25. In a relational database, a row or record is referred to as a(n)

    A. applet
    B. key field
    C. tuple
    D. bitmap

KEY (CORRECT ANSWERS)

1.	C	11.	D
2.	A	12.	B
3.	D	13.	B
4.	B	14.	D
5.	D	15.	D
6.	D	16.	B
7.	C	17.	B
8.	A	18.	B
9.	C	19.	C
10.	A	20.	D

21. A
22. C
23. C
24. A
25. C

TEST 2

DIRECTIONS: Each question or incomplete statement is followed by several suggested answers or completions. Select the one that BEST answers the question or completes the statement. *PRINT THE LETTER OF THE CORRECT ANSWER IN THE SPACE AT THE RIGHT.*

1. The technical staff of an organization are most likely to be users of a(n)   1.____

    A. transaction processing system (TPS)
    B. management information system (MIS)
    C. decision support system (DSS)
    D. knowledge work system (KWS)

2. The predefined packet of data in some LANs, which includes data indicating the sender, receiver, and whether the packet is in use, is known as a   2.____

    A. bus   B. check   C. token   D. parity

3. Which of the following is NOT a typical characteristic of hypertext and hypermedia applications?   3.____

    A. Users given commands to delete frames
    B. Independence from GUI environment
    C. Frames displayed in windows
    D. In shared systems, concurrent access to hypermedia data

4. Which of the following is a commercial digital information service that exists to provide business information?   4.____

    A. Prodigy   B. Dialog   C. Quotron   D. Lexis

5. Which of the following is NOT a characteristic of an enterprise MIS?   5.____

    A. Standardization
    B. Requires systems managers
    C. Homogeneous data
    D. Supports multiple applications

6. In workgroup information systems, the simplest type of group conferencing is referred to as a(n)   6.____

    A. videoconference   B. group meeting
    C. asynchronous meeting   D. electronic bulletin board

7. Which of the following is an advantage associated with the LAN model of multi-user systems?   7.____

    A. Reliability of many computers
    B. Unlimited performance
    C. Centralized control
    D. Relative independence from technology

8. The main advantage of digital private branch exchanges over other local networking options is that they   8.____

125

A. make use of existing phone lines
B. have a greater geographical range
C. perform important traffic control functions
D. can generally transmit larger volumes of data

9. In a typical organization, tactical and operational planning of an MIS would be the responsibility of the

   A. steering committee and MIS managers
   B. project teams
   C. operations personnel and end users
   D. chief information officer

9. _____

10. _____ code is the term for program instructions written in a high-level language before translation into machine language.

    A. Spaghetti   B. Source   C. Macro   D. Pseudo

10. _____

11. In its current form, the technology of electronic data interchange (EDI) is appropriate for transmitting all of the following EXCEPT

    A. purchase orders   B. bills of lading
    C. solicitations   D. invoices

11. _____

12. Which of the following types of applications is generally most dependent on the graphical user interface (GUI) environment?

    A. Electronic communication
    B. Desktop publishing
    C. Word processing
    D. Spreadsheet

12. _____

13. Which of the following is a logical design element of an information system?

    A. Hardware specifications   B. Output media
    C. Data models   D. Software

13. _____

14. A processing system rejects an order transaction for 10,000 units, on the basis that no order larger than 70 units had been placed previously. This is an example of a

    A. check digit   B. format check
    C. reasonableness check   D. dependency check

14. _____

15. The concentric circle on the surface area of a disk, on which data are stored as magnetized spots, is known as a

    A. cylinder   B. track   C. register   D. sector

15. _____

16. Which of the following storage media generally has the slowest access speed?

    A. Optical disk   B. RAM
    C. Magnetic disk   D. Cache

16. _____

17. The most time-consuming element of system conversion plans is

    A. hardware upgrading   B. personnel training
    C. documentation   D. data conversion

17. _____

18. In most organizations, the chief information officer is given a rank equivalent to

    A. project manager
    B. data administrator
    C. team leader
    D. vice president

19. Which of the following statements about the prototyping approach to systems development is FALSE?
    It is

    A. especially valuable for designing an end-user interface
    B. generally better suited for larger applications
    C. most useful when there is some uncertainty about requirements or design solutions
    D. as iterative process

20. What is the term for the final step in system reengineering, when the revised specifications are used to generate new, structure program code for a structured and maintainable system?

    A. Direct cutover
    B. Reverse engineering
    C. Workflow engineering
    D. Forward engineering

21. Which of the following are included in an MIS audit?
    I. Physical facilities
    II. Telecommunications
    III. Control systems
    IV. Manual procedures
    The CORRECT answer is:

    A. I, IV
    B. II, III
    C. I, II, III
    D. I, II, III, IV

22. In the traditional systems life cycle model, which of the following stages occurs EARLIEST?

    A. Programming
    B. Design
    C. Installation
    D. Systems study

23. Which of the following concerns is addressed by front-end CASE (Computer-Assisted Software Engineering) tools?

    A. Testing
    B. Analysis
    C. Maintenance
    D. Coding

24. In an individual MIS, the most commonly used analytical application is a

    A. statistical program
    B. gateway
    C. spreadsheet
    D. utility

25. Certain kinds of expert systems use the property of inheritance to organize and classify knowledge when the knowledge base is composed of easily identifiable chunks or objects of interrelated characteristics. These systems are known specifically as

    A. political models
    B. rule bases
    C. formal control tools
    D. semantic nets

KEY (CORRECT ANSWERS)

1. D
2. C
3. B
4. B
5. C

6. D
7. A
8. A
9. A
10. B

11. C
12. B
13. C
14. C
15. B

16. C
17. D
18. D
19. B
20. D

21. D
22. D
23. B
24. C
25. D

TEST 3

DIRECTIONS: Each question or incomplete statement is followed by several suggested answers or completions. Select the one that BEST answers the question or completes the statement. *PRINT THE LETTER OF THE CORRECT ANSWER IN THE SPACE AT THE RIGHT.*

1. Of an organization's total MIS budget, the majority can be expected to be spent on

   A. training
   B. programming
   C. operations
   D. administration

2. Each of the following is an element of the installation stage in the traditional model of a systems life cycle EXCEPT

   A. testing
   B. programming
   C. conversion
   D. training

3. For network applications in which some processing must be centralized and some can be performed locally, which of the following configurations is most appropriate?

   A. Bus   B. Ring   C. Star   D. Token ring

4. In systems development, the main difference between strategic analysis and enterprise analysis is that

   A. enterprise analysis makes use of the personal interview
   B. enterprise analysis produces a smaller data set
   C. strategic analysis is used exclusively in profit concerns
   D. strategic analysis tends to have a broader focus

5. Each of the following is a type of source data automation technology EXCEPT

   A. magnetic ink character recognition (MICR)
   B. touch screen
   C. bar code
   D. optical character recognition (OCR)

6. The main DISADVANTAGE associated with the parallel strategy of information system conversion is that

   A. run and personnel costs are extremely high
   B. it presents many difficulties in the area of documentation
   C. it provides no fallback in case of trouble
   D. it does not provide a clear picture of how the system will eventually operate throughout the entire organization

7. Which of the following types of systems is most appropriate for solving unstructured problems?

   A. Expert system
   B. Executive support system (ESS)
   C. Management information system (MIS)
   D. Decision support system (DSS)

8. In terms of information ethics, what is the term for the existence of laws that permit individuals to recover damages done to them by actors, systems, or organizations?

   A. Liability
   B. Subrogation
   C. Accountability
   D. Due process

9. Descriptions that focus on the dynamic aspects of a system's structure, or on change, evolution, and processes in general, are described as

   A. charismatic
   B. synchronic
   C. motile
   D. diachronic

10. One of the features of object-oriented programming is that all objects in a certain group have all the characteristics of that group. This feature is defined as

    A. base
    B. legitimacy
    C. class
    D. multiplexing

11. The most prominent data manipulation language in use today is

    A. Intellect
    B. Easytrieve
    C. APL
    D. SQL

12. Feasibility studies involved in systems analysis tend to focus on three specific areas. _____ feasibility is NOT one of these.

    A. Technical
    B. Operational
    C. Cultural
    D. Economic

13. A computer may sometimes handle programs more efficiently by dividing them into small fixed-or variable-length portions, with only a small portion stored in primary memory at one time. This is known as

    A. multitasking
    B. caching
    C. allocation
    D. virtual storage

14. Of the following applications, end-user computing is MOST appropriate for the development of

    A. scheduling systems for optimal production
    B. tracking daily trades of securities
    C. systems for handling air traffic
    D. systems for the development of three-dimensional graphics

15. In a hierarchical database, what is the term for the specialized data element attached to a record that shows the absolute or relative address of another record?

    A. Tickler   B. Index   C. Register   D. Pointer

16. For which of the following types of databases is the direct file access method most appropriate?

    A. Bank statements
    B. Payroll
    C. On-line hotel reservations
    D. Government benefits program

17. A _____ structured project with _____ technology requirements would most likely involve the lowest degree of risk to an organization.

    A. small, highly; low
    B. small, flexibly; high
    C. large, flexibly; high
    D. large, highly; low

18. Historically, under federal law creators of intellectual property were protected against copying by others for a period of

    A. 10 years
    B. 17 years
    C. 28 years
    D. the creator's natural life

19. Most modern secondary storage devices operate at speeds measured in

    A. nanoseconds
    B. milliseconds
    C. microseconds
    D. seconds

20. Which of the following signifies the international standard for transmitting voice, video, and data to support a wide range of service over the public telephone lines?

    A. HTML   B. ISDN   C. TCP/IP   D. ASCII

21. An important limitation associated with executive support systems today is that they

    A. use data from different systems designed for very different purposes
    B. have a narrow range of easy-to-use desktop analytical tools
    C. are used almost exclusively by executives
    D. do an inadequate job of filtering data

22. Each of the following is an element of the systems study stage in the traditional model of a systems life cycle EXCEPT

    A. identifying objectives to be attained by a solution
    B. determining whether the organization has a problem that can be solved with a system
    C. analyzing problems with existing systems
    D. describing alternative solutions

23. The commercial software product *Lotus Notes* is an example of

    A. intelligent agent software
    B. groupware
    C. a star network
    D. electronic data interchange (EDI)

24. Weaknesses in a system's _____ controls may create errors or failures in new or modified systems.

    A. data file security
    B. implementation
    C. physical hardware
    D. software

25. Which of the following is a term used to describe the ability to move from summary data to more specific levels of detail?   25._____

   A. Drill down
   B. Forward chaining
   C. Downsizing
   D. Semantic networking

KEY (CORRECT ANSWERS)

1. C
2. B
3. C
4. D
5. B

6. A
7. B
8. A
9. D
10. C

11. D
12. C
13. D
14. D
15. D

16. C
17. A
18. C
19. B
20. B

21. A
22. B
23. B
24. B
25. A

EXAMINATION SECTION
TEST 1

DIRECTIONS: Each question or incomplete statement is followed by several suggested answers or completions. Select the one that BEST answers the question or completes the statement. *PRINT THE LETTER OF THE CORRECT ANSWER IN THE SPACE AT THE RIGHT.*

1. Which of the following words in a pseudocode statement can be replaced by the word *read?*

    A. Get   B. Print   C. Set   D. Store

    1.____

2. Units of input and output in pseudocode are known as

    A. lines   B. items   C. strings   D. records

    2.____

3. The statement required to print the value of number of students followed by the label PEOPLE would be written:

    A. Set value to PEOPLE
    B. Print *number of students* and PEOPLE
    C. Read *number of students* and PEOPLE
    D. Write *number of students* and PEOPLE

    3.____

4. What command word is used to save contents of another storage location or a constant in a storage location?

    A. Store   B. Set   C. Get   D. Put

    4.____

5. The symbol used for multiplication in pseudocode is

    A.   B. /   C. *   D. x

    5.____

6. A statement constructed to give the first number in a data set the same value as the second number would be expressed as _____ first number _____ second number.

    A. read; as   B. set; to
    C. declare; as   D. —; =

    6.____

7. The function of a literal is to

    A. read stored values
    B. identify or describe output
    C. write results
    D. store input values

    7.____

8. What is the term for a grouping of items that have a similar characteristic or common identifying property?

    A. Set   B. Array
    C. String   D. Assortment

    8.____

9. When calculations are written in algebraic expression, the name of the storage location in which the result would be *save* is expressed as

    A. zero   B. =   C. x   D. y

    9.____

10. If a value of 10 is stored in memory at X, the output that the statement *Print 'X'* would produce is

    A. 10 B. 'X' C. X D. X = 10

11. Which of the following steps in using a subprogram would occur FIRST?

    A. Subprogram executed
    B. Subprogram invoked
    C. Program continues execution
    D. Results passed through program

12. A declaration for the data item *inventory item stock number* would be written: Declare

    A. stock number, numeric inventory item
    B. numeric inventory item stock number
    C. inventory item stock number
    D. character inventory item stock number

13. Of the following, a(n) _____ is NOT always an element of the *loop while* construct.

    A. *end loop* statement
    B. counter
    C. group of one or more statements forming the loop body
    D. means of making the *loop while* condition false

14. Information is placed into a storage location by means of a(n) _____ statement.

    A. call B. assignment
    C. return D. address

15. A programmer wants to place a zero into a memory location that is to contain a counter. Each of the following is a possible statement EXCEPT:

    A. Set counter to zero
    B. Initialize zero in counter
    C. Set COUNT to zero
    D. Store zero in counter

16. What is the term used for the items of information necessary for a program or subprogram to perform its task?

    A. Records B. Functions
    C. Parameters D. Constructs

17. Which of the following items of input would be needed in order to construct a module that finds the sum of two arrays, A and B?
    The

    A. number of elements in A and B
    B. loop for J = 1 to the number of elements in A and B
    C. two numbers, J and K
    D. sum of the two arrays

18. A statement constructed to initialize a total cost at zero would be written: 18.____

    A. Set total cost to zero   B. Set zero to total cost
    C. Total cost =0   D. Read total cost as zero

19. In order to provide a means of executing a named block of statements, the _____ is used. 19.____

    A. call statement   B. selection parameter
    C. return statement   D. do module

20. Each element in an array is identified by a number called a _____, which designates position in the array. 20.____

    A. marker   B. literal
    C. string   D. subscript

21. A value of 8 is stored in memory at X.
    The following statement would produce the output X = 8. 21.____

    A. Print X = 8   B. Read X as 8
    C. Print 'X =' and X   D. Print 'X = 8'

22. The symbol for division in pseudocode is 22.____

    A. —   B. ∫   C. ÷   D. /

23. A data item is denoted as non-numeric by means of a(n) 23.____

    A. record   B. string   C. address   D. name

24. A statement constructed to set the value of an employee count to zero would be written: 24.____

    A. Get zero employee count
    B. Read zero for employee count
    C. Set employee count to zero
    D. Put employee count at zero

25. Which of the following key words is NOT used for the purpose of selection in pseudocode? 25.____

    A. Else   B. Then   C. While   D. If

KEY (CORRECT ANSWERS)

1.	A	11.	B
2.	D	12.	D
3.	D	13.	B
4.	B	14.	B
5.	C	15.	B
6.	B	16.	C
7.	B	17.	A
8.	B	18.	A
9.	C	19.	D
10.	C	20.	D

21. C
22. D
23. B
24. C
25. C

TEST 2

DIRECTIONS: Each question or incomplete statement is followed by several suggested answers or completions. Select the one that BEST answers the question or completes the statement. *PRINT THE LETTER OF THE CORRECT ANSWER IN THE SPACE AT THE RIGHT.*

1. To perform loop operation, each of the following must be done to the counter EXCEPT   1.____

    A. division   B. initialization
    C. testing   D. incrementation

2. A subprogram that finds the largest element in an array can be constructed as a   2.____

    A. loop   B. function
    C. loop with counter   D. do module

3. *Read employee's name, hourly pay rate, number of hours worked, and gross pay.*   3.____
   In the above statement, the optional word is

    A. rate   B. and   C. number   D. read

4. *Find degrees Fahrenheit by multiplying degrees centigrade by nine-fifths and adding 32 to the result.*   4.____
   To compute and save the result for the above, the required statement using algebraic form would be written:

    A. F = ((9*C)/5) + 32
    B. F = (9/5)xC) + 32
    C. Set F to ((9.C/5) + 32
    D. F = 9/5C + 32

5. Output in pseudocode is indicated by each of the following key words EXCEPT   5.____

    A. print   B. get   C. write   D. put

6. The _____ statement is placed at the bottom of a selection group.   6.____

    A. call   B. return   C. do   D. end if

7. A statement constructed to save 100 in number of people would be written: 7.____

    A. Read 100 for number of people
    B. Store 100 for number of people
    C. Set 100 for number of people
    D. Set number of people to 100

8. In pseudocode, the *loop with counter* construct is specified by the key words   8.____

    A. loop while   B. end loop
    C. loop for   D. end if

9. A programmer wishes to construct a nested selection to handle the following case: Add 1 to senior resident counter when town residence is Oakville and person's age is greater than 64.   9.____
   In the best logical construction, the statement would begin:

137

A. Others counter = others counter + 1
B. If town of residence is Oakville
C. If age is greater than 64
D. Senior residence counter = senior resident counter + 1

10. Which of the following terms is NOT used to indicate the meaning of output in pseudocode?

    A. Character string
    B. Label
    C. Record
    D. Literal

11. What kind of statement is used to revert control to a calling program?

    A. Call
    B. End loop
    C. Return
    D. Reassignment

12. The statement required to save the literal SUSPENDED in student status would be written:

    A. Write student status as SUSPENDED
    B. Get SUSPENDED to student status
    C. Set student status to 'SUSPENDED'
    D. Read student status as 'SUSPENDED'

13. Which of the following words in a pseudocode statement can be replaced by the word *print*?

    A. Get
    B. Print
    C. Set
    D. Store

14. In pseudocode, the = symbol indicates

    A. division
    B. an equality of values
    C. a read command
    D. a storage assignment for information

15. Which of the following steps in using a subprogram would occur LAST?

    A. Subprogram executed
    B. Subprogram invoked
    C. Program continues execution
    D. Results passed through program

16. If a value of 10 is stored in memory at X, the statement *Print X* will produce the output

    A. 10
    B. 'X'
    C. X
    D. X = 10

17. Which of the following is NOT an example of a non-numeric data item?

    A. Telephone number
    B. ZIP code
    C. Student identification number
    D. Temperature

18. For moving the contents of one storage location to another location in algebraic expression, a statement of the form _____ should be used.

    A. x = y
    B. Move x to y
    C. x/y
    D. Set x to y

19. A declaration for the data item *number of employees* would be written: Declare

    A. employees, number of
    B. numeric number of employees
    C. number of employees
    D. character number of employees

20. In a *loop while* construct, the loop will be terminated upon the introduction of a(n)

    A. false condition
    B. return statement
    C. subprogram
    D. *end if* statement

21. The statement required to print the message GROSS PAY IS $ followed by the value of gross pay would be written:

    A. Get gross pay and GROSS PAY IS $
    B. Read 'GROSS PAY IS $' and gross pay
    C. Write 'GROSS PAY IS $' and gross pay
    D. Print 'GROSS PAY IS $' and gross pay

22. In pseudocode, the value x^2 would be written

    A. X-2
    B. X**2
    C. X//2
    D. X*2

23. A statement using algebraic form to compute and save the result for *Add one to number of days* would be written:

    A. Number of days + 1
    B. Number of days = number of days + 1
    C. Set number of days to number of days + 1
    D. Set number of days + 1

24. What type of statement is used to invoke a subprogram?

    A. Do
    B. Call
    C. Assignment
    D. Return

25. A programmer wants to construct a statement that instructs the computer to print the message *There is no sales tax* if the tax code is zero and *The sales tax is 4%* otherwise. In the statement, what would follow the key word *else*?

    A. Write 'There is no sales tax'
    B. Get tax code
    C. Write 'The sales tax is 4%'
    D. Set tax code to zero

4 (#2)

KEY (CORRECT ANSWERS)

1.	A	11.	C
2.	B	12.	C
3.	B	13.	B
4.	A	14.	D
5.	B	15.	C
6.	D	16.	A
7.	D	17.	D
8.	C	18.	A
9.	C	19.	B
10.	C	20.	A

21. C
22. B
23. B
24. B
25. C

PREPARING WRITTEN MATERIAL

PARAGRAPH REARRANGEMENT
COMMENTARY

The sentences that follow are in scrambled order. You are to rearrange them in proper order and indicate the letter choice containing the correct answer at the space at the right.

Each group of sentences in this section is actually a paragraph presented in scrambled order. Each sentence in the group has a place in that paragraph; no sentence is to be left out. You are to read each group of sentences and decide upon the best order in which to put the sentences so as to form a well-organized paragraph.

The questions in this section measure the ability to solve a problem when all the facts relevant to its solution are not given.

More specifically, certain positions of responsibility and authority require the employee to discover connection between events sometimes, apparently, unrelated. In order to do this, the employee will find it necessary to correctly infer that unspecified events have probably occurred or are likely to occur. This ability becomes especially important when action must be taken on incomplete information.

Accordingly, these questions require competitors to choose among several suggested alternatives, each of which presents a different sequential arrangement of the events. Competitors must choose the MOST logical of the suggested sequences.

In order to do so, they may be required to draw on general knowledge to infer missing concepts or events that are essential to sequencing the given events. Competitors should be careful to infer only what is essential to the sequence. The plausibility of the wrong alternatives will always require the inclusion of unlikely events or of additional chains of events which are NOT essential to sequencing the given events.

It's very important to remember that you are looking for the best of the four possible choices, and that the best choice of all may not even be one of the answers you're given to choose from.

There is no one right way to solve these problems. Many people have found it helpful to first write out the order of the sentences, as they would have arranged them, on their scrap paper before looking at the possible answers. If their optimum answer is there, this can save them some time. If it isn't, this method can still give insight into solving the problem. Others find it most helpful to just go through each of the possible choices, contrasting each as they go along. You should use whatever method feels comfortable and works for you.

While most of these types of questions are not that difficult, we've added a higher percentage of the difficult type, just to give you more practice. Usually there are only one or two questions on this section that contain such subtle distinctions that you're unable to answer confidently. And you then may find yourself stuck deciding between two possible choices, neither of which you're sure about.

EXAMINATION SECTION

TEST 1

DIRECTIONS: The following groups of sentences need to be arranged in an order that makes sense. Select the letter preceding the sequence that represents the BEST sentence order. *PRINT THE LETTER OF THE CORRECT ANSWER IN THE SPACE AT THE RIGHT.*

1.
   I. The keyboard was purposely designed to be a little awkward to slow typists down.
   II. The arrangement of letters on the keyboard of a typewriter was not designed for the convenience of the typist.
   III. Fortunately, no one is suggesting that a new keyboard be designed right away.
   IV. If one were, we would have to learn to type all over again.
   V. The reason was that the early machines were slower than the typists and would jam easily.
   The CORRECT answer is:
   A. I, III, IV, II, V   B. II, V, I, IV, III
   C. V, I, II, III, IV   D. II, I, V, III, IV

   1.____

2.
   I. The majority of the new service jobs are part-time or low-paying.
   II. According to the U.S. Bureau of Labor Statistics, jobs in the service sector constitute 72% of all jobs in this country.
   III. If more and more workers receive less and less money, who will buy the goods and services needed to keep the economy going?
   IV. The service sector is by far the fastest growing part of the United States economy.
   V. Some economists look upon this trend with great concern.
   The CORRECT answer is:
   A. II, IV, I, V, III   B. II, III, IV, I, V
   C. V, IV, II, III, I   D. III, I, II, IV, V

   2.____

3.
   I. They can also affect one's endurance.
   II. This can stabilize blood sugar levels, and ensure that the brain is receiving a steady, constant, supply of glucose, so that one is *hitting on all cylinders* while taking the test.
   III. By food, we mean real food, not junk food or unhealthy snacks.
   IV. For this reason, it is important not to skip a meal, and to bring food with you to the exam.
   V. One's blood sugar levels can affect how clearly one is able to think and concentrate during an exam.
   The CORRECT answer is:
   A. V, IV, II, III, I   B. V, II, I, IV, III
   C. V, I, IV, III, II   D. V, IV, I, III, II

   3.____

4. I. Those who are the embodiment of desire are absorbed in material quests, and those who are the embodiment of feeling are warriors who value power more than possession.
II. These qualities are in everyone, but in different degrees.
III. But those who value understanding yearn not for goods or victory, but for knowledge.
IV. According to Plato, human behavior flows from three main sources: desire, emotion, and knowledge.
V. In the perfect state, the industrial forces would produce but not rule, the military would protect but not rule, and the forces of knowledge, the philosopher kings, would reign.

The CORRECT answer is:
A. IV, V, I, II, III
B. V, I, II, III, IV
C. IV, III, II, I, V
D. IV, II, I, III, V

5. I. Of the more than 26,000 tons of garbage produced daily in New York City, 12,000 tons arrive daily at Fresh Kills.
II. In a month, enough garbage accumulates there to fill the Empire State Building.
III. In 1937, the Supreme Court halted the practice of dumping the trash of New York City into the sea.
IV. Although the garbage is compacted, in a few years the mounds of garbage at Fresh Kills will be the highest points south of Maine's Mount Desert Island on the Eastern Seaboard.
V. Instead, tugboats now pull barges of much of the trash to Staten Island and the largest landfill in the world, Fresh Kills.

The CORRECT answer is:
A. III, V, IV, I, II
B. III, V, II, IV, I
C. III, V, I, II, IV
D. III, II, V, IV, I

6. I. Communists rank equality very high, but freedom very low.
II. Unlike communists, conservatives place a high value on freedom and a very low value on equality.
III. A recent study demonstrated that one way to classify people's political beliefs is to look at the importance placed on two words: freedom and equality.
IV. Thus, by demonstrating how members of these groups feel about the two words, the study has proved to be useful for political analysts in several European countries.
V. According to the study, socialists and liberals rank both freedom and equality very high, while fascists rate both very low.

The CORRECT answer is:
A. III, V, I, II, IV
B. V, IV, III, I, II
C. III, V, IV, II, I
D. III, I, II, IV, V

7. I. "Can there be anything more amazing than this?"
    II. If the riddle is successfully answered, his dead brothers will be brought back to life.
    III. "Even though man sees those around him dying every day," says Dharmaraj, "he still believes and acts as if he were immortal."
    IV. "What is the cause of ceaseless wonder?" asks the Lord of the Lake.
    V. In the ancient epic, The Mahabharata, a riddle is asked of one of the Pandava brothers.
    The CORRECT answer is:
    A. V, II, I, IV, III
    B. V, IV, III, I, II
    C. V, II, IV, III, I
    D. V, II, IV, I, III

8. I. On the contrary, the two main theories—the cooperative (neoclassical) theory and the radical (labor theory)—clearly rest on very different assumptions, which have very different ethical overtones.
    II. The distribution of income is the primary factor in determining the relative levels of material well-being that different groups or individuals attain.
    III. Of all issues in economics, the distribution of income is one of the most controversial.
    IV. The neoclassical theory tends to support the existing income distribution (or minor changes), while the labor theory ends to support substantial changes in the way income is distributed.
    V. The intensity of the controversy reflects the fact that different economic theories are not purely neutral, *detached* theories with no ethical or moral implications.
    The CORRECT answer is:
    A. II, I, V, IV, III
    B. III, II, V, I, IV
    C. III, V, II, I, IV
    D. III, V, IV, I, II

9. I. The pool acts as a broker and ensures that the cheapest power gets used first.
    II. Every six seconds, the pool's computer monitors all of the generating stations in the state and decides which to ask for more power and which to cut back.
    III. The buying and selling of electrical power is handled by the New York Power Pool in Guilderland, New York.
    IV. This is to the advantage of both the buying and selling utilities.
    V. The pool began operation in 1970, and consists of the state's eight electric utilities.
    The CORRECT answer is:
    A. V, I, II, III, IV
    B. IV, II, I, III, V
    C. III, V, I, IV, II
    D. V, III, IV, II, I

10.
I. Modern English is much simpler grammatically than Old English.
II. Finnish grammar is very complicated; there are some fifteen cases, for example.
III. Chinese, a very old language, may seem to be the exception, but it is the great number of characters/words that must be mastered that makes it so difficult to learn, not its grammar.
IV. The newest literary language—that is, written as well as spoken—is Finish, whose literary roots go back only to about the middle of the nineteenth century.
V. Contrary to popular belief, the longer a language is been in use the simpler its grammar—not the reverse.

The CORRECT answer is:
A. IV, I, II, III, V
B. V, I, IV, II, III
C. I, II, IV, III, V
D. IV, II, III, I, V

10.____

KEY (CORRECT ANSWERS)

1. D   6. A
2. A   7. C
3. C   8. B
4. D   9. C
5. C   10. B

TEST 2

DIRECTIONS: This type of question tests your ability to recognize accurate paraphrasing, well-constructed paragraphs, and appropriate style and tone. It is important that the answer you select contains only the facts or concepts given in the original sentences. It is also important that you be aware of incomplete sentences, inappropriate transitions, unsupported opinions, incorrect usage, and illogical sentence order. Paragraphs that do not include all the necessary facts and concepts, that distort them, or that add new ones are not considered correct.

The format for this section may vary. Sometimes, long paragraphs are given, and emphasis is placed on style and organization. Our first five questions are of this type. Other times, the paragraphs are shorter, and there is less emphasis on style and more emphasis on accurate representation of information. Our second group of five questions are of this nature.

For each of Questions 1 through 10, select the paragraph that BEST expresses the ideas contained in the sentences above it. *PRINT THE LETTER OF THE CORRECT ANSWER IN THE SPACE AT THE RIGHT.*

1. I. Listening skills are very important for managers.
    II. Listening skills are not usually emphasized.
    III. Whenever managers are depicted in books, manuals or the media, they are always talking, never listening.
    IV. We'd like you to read the enclosed handout on listening skills and to try to consciously apply them this week.
    V. We guarantee they will improve the quality of your interactions.

    1.____

    A. Unfortunately, listening skills are not usually emphasized for managers. Managers are always depicted as talking, never listening. We'd like you to read the enclosed handout on listening skills. Please try to apply these principles this week. If you do, we guarantee they will improve the quality of your interactions.
    B. The enclosed handout on listening skills will be important improving the quality of your interactions. We guarantee it. All you have to do is take sometime this week to read and to consciously try to apply the principles. Listening skills are very important for manages, but they are not usually emphasized. Whenever managers are depicted in books, manuals or the media, they are always talking, never listening.
    C. Listening well is one of the most important skills a manager can have, yet it's not usually given much attention. Think about any representation of managers in books, manuals, or in the media that you may have seen. They're always talking, never listening. We'd like you to read the enclosed handout on listening skills and consciously try to apply them the rest of the week. We guarantee you will see a difference in the quality of your interactions.

147

D. Effective listening, one very important tool in the effective manager's arsenal, is usually not emphasized enough. The usual depiction of managers in books, manuals or the media is one in which they are always talking, never listening. We'd like you to read the enclosed handout and consciously try to apply the information contained therein throughout the rest of the week. We feel sure that you will see a marked difference in the quality of your interactions.

2.
I. Chekhov wrote three dramatic masterpieces which share certain themes and formats: Uncle Vanya, The Cherry Orchard, and The Three Sisters.
II. They are primarily concerned with the passage of time and how this erodes human aspirations.
III. The plays are haunted by the ghosts of the wasted life.
IV. The characters are concerned with life's lesser problems; however, such as the inability to make decisions, loyalty to the wrong cause, and the inability to be clear.
V. This results in sweet, almost aching, type of a sadness referred to as Chekhovian.

2.____

    A. Chekhov wrote three dramatic masterpieces: Uncle Vanya, The Cherry Orchard, and The Three Sisters. These masterpieces share certain themes and formats: the passage of time, how time erodes human aspirations, and the ghosts of wasted life. Each masterpiece is characterized by a sweet, almost aching, type of sadness that has become known as Chekhovian. The sweetness of this sadness hinges on the fact that it is not the great tragedies of life which are destroying these characters, but their minor flaws: indecisiveness, misplaced loyalty, unclarity.

    B. The Cherry Orchard, Uncle Vanya, and The Three Sisters are three dramatic masterpieces written by Chekhov that use similar formats to explore a common theme. Each is primarily concerned with the way that passing time wears down human aspirations, and each is haunted by the ghosts of the wasted life. The characters are shown struggling futilely with the lesser problems of life: indecisiveness, loyalty to the wrong cause, and the inability to be clear. These struggles create a mood of sweet, almost aching, sadness that has become known as Chekhovian.

    C. Chekhov's dramatic masterpieces are, along with The Cherry Orchard, Uncle Vanya, and The Three Sisters. These plays share certain thematic and formal similarities. They are concerned most of all with the passage of time and the way in which time erodes human aspirations. Each play is haunted by the specter of the wasted life. Chekhov's characters are caught, however, by life's lesser snares: indecisiveness, loyalty to the wrong cause, and unclarity. The characteristic mood is a sweet, almost aching type of sadness that has come to be known as Chekhovian.

    D. A Chekhovian mood is characterized by sweet, almost aching, sadness. The term comes from three dramatic tragedies by Chekhov which revolve around the sadness of a wasted life. The three masterpieces (Uncle Vanya, The Three Sisters, and The Cherry Orchard) share the same theme and format. The plays are concerned with how the passage of time erodes human aspirations. They are peopled with characters who are struggling with life's lesser problems. These are people who are indecisive, loyal to the wrong causes, or are unable to make themselves clear.

3.
 I. Movie previews have often helped producers decide which parts of movies they should take out or leave in.
 II. The first 1933 preview of King Kong was very helpful to the producers because many people ran screaming from the theater and would not return when four men first attacked by Kong were eaten by giant spiders.
 III. The 1950 premiere of Sunset Boulevard resulted in the filming of an entirely new beginning, and a delay of six months in the film's release.
 IV. In the original opening scene, William Holden was in a morgue talking with thirty-six other "corpses" about the ways some of them had died.
 V. When he began to tell them of his life with Gloria Swanson, the audience found this hilarious, instead of taking the scene seriously.

3.____

 A. Movie previews have often helped producers decide what parts of movies they should leave in or take out. For example, the first preview of King Kong in 1933 was very helpful. In one scene, four men were first attacked by Kong and then eaten by giant spiders. Many members of the audience ran screaming from the theater and would not return. The premiere of the 1950 film Sunset Boulevard was also very helpful. In the original opening scene, William Holden was in a morgue with thirty-six other "corpses," discussing the ways some of them had died. When he began to tell them of his life with Gloria Swanson, the audience found this hilarious. They were supposed to take the scene seriously. The result was a delay of six months in the release of the film while a new beginning was added.
 B. Movie previews have often helped producers decide whether they should change various parts of a movie. After the 1933 preview of King Kong, a scene in which four men who had been attacked by Kong were eaten by giant spiders was taken out as many people ran screaming from the theater and would not return. The 1950 premiere of Sunset Boulevard also led to some changes. In the original opening scene, William Holden was in a morgue talking with thirty-six other "corpses" about the ways some of them had died. When he began to tell them of his life with Gloria Swanson, the audience found this hilarious, instead of taking the scene seriously.
 C. What do Sunset Boulevard and King Kong have in common? Both show the value of using movie previews to test audience reaction. The first 1933 preview of King Kong showed that a scene showing four men being eaten by giant spiders after having been attacked by Kong was too frightening for many people. They ran screaming from the theater and couldn't be coaxed back. The 1950 premiere of Sunset Boulevard was also a scream, but not the kind the producers intended. The movie opens

with William Holden lying in a morgue discussing the ways they had died with thirty-six other "corpses." When he began to tell them of his life with Gloria Swanson, the audience couldn't take him seriously. Their laughter caused a six-month delay while the beginning was rewritten.

D. Producers very often use movie previews to decide if changes are needed. The premiere of <u>Sunset Boulevard</u> in 1950 led to a new beginning and a six-month delay in film release. At the beginning, William Holden and thirty-six other "corpses" discuss the ways some of them died. Rather than taking this seriously, the audience thought it was hilarious when he began to tell them of his life with Gloria Swanson. The first 1933 preview of <u>King Kong</u> was very helpful for its producers because one scene so terrified the audience that many of them ran screaming from the theater and would not return. In this particular scene, four men who had first been attacked by Kong were eaten by giant spiders.

4.
I. It is common for supervisors to view employees as "things" to be manipulated.
II. This approach does not motivate employees, nor does the carrot-and-stick approach because employees often recognize these behaviors and resent them.
III. Supervisors can change these behaviors by using self-inquiry and persistence.
IV. The best managers genuinely respect those they work with, are supportive and helpful, and are interested in working as a team with those they supervise.
V. They disagree with the Golden Rule that says "he or she who has the gold makes the rules."

4._____

A. Some managers act as if they think the Golden Rule means "he or she who has the gold makes the rules." They show disrespect to employees by seeing them as "things" to be manipulated. Obviously, this approach does not motivate employees any more than the carrot-and-stick approach motivates them. The employees are smart enough to spot these behaviors and resent them. On the other hand, the managers genuinely respect those they work with, are supportive and helpful, and are interested in working as a team. Self-inquiry and persistence can change even the former type of supervisor into the latter.

B. Many supervisors all into the trap of viewing employees as "things" to be manipulated, or try to motivate them by using a carrot-and-stick approach. These methods do not motivate employees, who often recognize the behaviors and resent them. Supervisors can change these behaviors, however, by using self-inquiry and persistence. The best managers are supportive and helpful, and have genuine respect for those with whom they work. They are interested in working as a team with those they supervise. To them, the Golden Rule is not "he or she who has the gold makes the rules."

C. Some supervisors see employees as "things" to be used or manipulated using a carrot-and-stick technique. These methods don't work. Employees often see through them and resent them. A supervisor who wants to change may do so. The techniques of self-inquiry and persistence can be used to turn him or her into the type of supervisor who doesn't think the Golden Rule is "he or she who has the gold makes the rules." They may become like the best managers who treat those with whom they work with respect and give them help and support. These are the manager who know how to build a team.

D. Unfortunately, many supervisors act as if their employees are objects whose movements they can position at will. This mistaken belief has the same result as another popular motivational technique—the carrot-and-stick approach. Both attitudes can lead to the same result—resentment from those employees who recognize the behaviors for what they are. Supervisors who recognize these behaviors can change through the use of persistence and the use of self-inquiry. It's important to remember that the best managers respect their employees. They readily give necessary help and support and are interested in working as a team with those they supervise. To these managers, the Golden Rule is not "he or she who has the gold makes the rules."

5. I. The first half of the nineteenth century produced a group of pessimistic poets—Byron, De Musset, Heine, Pushkin, and Leopardi.
    II. It also produced a group of pessimistic composers—Schubert, Chopin, Schumann, and even the later Beethoven.
    III. Above all, in philosophy, there was the profoundly pessimistic philosopher, Schopenhauer.
    IV. The Revolution was dead, the Bourbons were restored, the feudal barons were reclaiming their land, and progress everywhere was being suppressed, as the great age was over.
    V. "I thank God," said Goethe, "that I am not young in so thoroughly finished a world."

    A. "I thank God," said Goethe, "that I am not young in so thoroughly finished a world." The Revolution was dead, the Bourbons were restored, the feudal barons were reclaiming their land, and progress everywhere was being suppressed. The first half of the nineteenth century produced a group of pessimistic poets: Byron, De Musset, Heine, Pushkin, and Leopardi. It also produced pessimistic composers: Schubert, Chopin, Schumann. Although Beethoven came later, he fits into this group, too. Finally and above all, it also produced a profoundly pessimistic philosopher, Schopenhauer. The great age was over.
    B. The first half of the nineteenth century produced a group of pessimistic poets: Byron, De Musset, Heine, Pushkin, and Leopardi. It produced a group of pessimistic composers: Schubert, Chopin, Schumann, and even the later Beethoven. Above all, it produced a profoundly pessimistic philosopher, Schopenhauer. For each of these men, the great age was over. The Revolution was dead, and the Bourbons were restored. The feudal barons were reclaiming their land, and progress everywhere was being suppressed.

5.____

C. The great age was over. The Revolution was dead—the Bourbons were restored, and the feudal barons were reclaiming their land. Progress everywhere was being suppressed. Out of this climate came a profound pessimism. Poets, like Byron, De Musset, Heine, Pushkin, and Leopardi; composers, like Schubert, Chopin, Schumann, and even the later Beethoven; and above all, a profoundly pessimistic philosopher, Schopenauer. This pessimism which arose in the first half of the nineteenth century is illustrated by these words of Goethe, "I thank God that I am not young in so thoroughly finished a world."
D. The first half of the nineteenth century produced a group of pessimistic poets, Byron, De Musset, Heine, Pushkin, and Leopardi—and a group of pessimistic composers, Schubert, Chopin, Schumann, and the later Beethoven. Above it all, it produced a profoundly pessimistic philosopher, Schopenhauer. The great age was over. The Revolution was dead, the Bourbons were restored, the feudal barons were reclaiming their land, and progress everywhere was being suppressed. "I thank God," said Goethe, "that I am not young in so thoroughly finished a world."

6. I. A new manager sometimes may feel insecure about his or her competence in the new position.
    II. The new manager may then exhibit defensive or arrogant behavior towards those one supervises, or the new manager may direct overly flattering behavior toward one's new supervisor.

    A. Sometimes, a new manager may feel insecure about his or her ability to perform well in this new position. The insecurity may lead him or her to treat others differently. He or she may display arrogant or defensive behavior towards those he or she supervises, or be overly flattering to his or her new supervisor.
    B. A new manager may sometimes feel insecure about his or her ability to perform well in the new position. He or she may then become arrogant, defensive, or overly flattering towards those he or she works with.
    C. There are times when a new manager may be insecure about how well he or she can perform in the new job. The new manager may also behave defensive or act in an arrogant way towards those he or she supervises, or overly flatter his or her boss.
    D. Sometimes a new manager may feel insecure about his or her ability to perform well in the new position. He or she may then display arrogant or defensive behavior towards those they supervise, or become overly flattering towards their supervisors.

7. I. It is possible to eliminate unwanted behavior by bringing it under stimulus control—tying the behavior to a cue, and then never, or rarely, giving the cue.
    II. One trainer successfully used this method to keep an energetic young porpoise from coming out of her tank whenever she felt like it, which was potentially dangerous.
    III. Her trainer taught her to do it for a reward, in response to a hand signal, and then rarely gave the signal.

A. Unwanted behavior can be eliminated by tying the behavior to a cue, and then never, or rarely, giving the cue. This is called stimulus control. One trainer was able to use this method to keep an energetic young porpoise from coming out of her tank by teaching her to come out for a reward in response to a hand signal, and then rarely giving the signal.

B. Stimulus control can be used to eliminate unwanted behavior. In this method, behavior is tied to a cue, and then the cue is rarely, if ever, given. One trainer was able to successfully use stimulus control to keep an energetic young porpoise from coming out of her tank whenever she felt like it—a potentially dangerous practice. She taught the porpoise to come out for a reward when she gave a hand signal, and then rarely gave the signal.

C. It is possible to eliminate behavior that is undesirable by bringing it under stimulus control by tying behavior to a signal, and then rarely giving the signal. One trainer successfully used this method to keep an energetic porpoise from coming out of her tank, a potentially dangerous situation. Her trainer taught the porpoise to do it for a reward, in response to a hand signal, and then would rarely give the signal.

D. By using stimulus control, it is possible to eliminate unwanted behavior by tying the behavior to a cue, and then rarely or never give the cue. One trainer was able to use this method to successfully stop a young porpoise from coming out of her tank whenever she felt like it. To curb this potentially dangerous practice, the porpoise was taught by the trainer to come out of the tank for a reward, in response to a hand signal, and then rarely given the signal.

8. I. There is a great deal of concern over the safety of commercial trucks, caused by their greatly increased role in serious accidents since federal deregulation in 1981.
    II. Recently, 60 percent of trucks in New York and Connecticut and 70 percent of trucks in Maryland randomly stopped by state troopers failed safety inspections.
    III. Sixteen states in the United States require no training at all for truck drivers.

    A. Since federal deregulation in 1981, there has been a great deal of concern over the safety of commercial trucks, and their greatly increased role in serious accidents. Recently, 60 percent of trucks in New York and Connecticut, and 70 percent of trucks in Maryland failed safety inspections. Sixteen states in the United States require no training at all for truck drivers.
    B. There is a great deal of concern over the safety of commercial trucks since federal deregulation in 1981. Their role in serious accidents has greatly increased. Recently, 60 percent of trucks randomly stopped in Connecticut and New York and 70 percent in Maryland failed safety inspections conducted by state troopers. Sixteen states in the United States provide no training at all for truck drivers.
    C. Commercial trucks have a greatly increased role in serious accidents since federal deregulation in 1981. This has led to a great deal of concern.

8.____

Recently, 70 percent of trucks in Maryland and 60 percent of trucks in New York and Connecticut failed inspection of those that were randomly stopped by state troopers. Sixteen states in the United States require no training for all truck drivers.

D. Since federal deregulation in 1981, the role that commercial trucks have played in serious accidents has greatly increased, and this has led to a great deal of concern. Recently, 60 percent of trucks in New York and Connecticut, and 70 percent of trucks in Maryland randomly stopped by state troopers failed safety inspections. Sixteen states in the U.S. don't require any training for truck drivers.

9.
I. No matter how much some people have, they still feel unsatisfied and want more, or want to keep what they have forever.
II. One recent television documentary showed several people flying from New York to Paris for a one-day shopping spree to buy platinum earrings, because they were bored.
III. In Brazil, some people were ordering coffins that cost a minimum of $45,000 and are equipping them with deluxe stereos, televisions, and other graveyard necessities.

9.____

A. Some people, despite having a great deal, still feel unsatisfied and want more, or think they can keep what they have forever. One recent documentary on television showed several people enroute from Paris to New York for a one day shopping spree to buy platinum earrings, because they were bored. Some people in Brazil are even ordering coffins equipped with such graveyard necessities as deluxe stereos and televisions. The price of the coffins start at $45,000.
B. No matter how much some people have, they may feel unsatisfied. This leads them to want more, or to want to keep what they have forever. Recently, a television documentary depicting several people flying from New York to Paris for a one day shopping spree to buy platinum earrings. They were bored. Some people in Brazil are ordering coffins that cost at least $45,000 and come equipped with deluxe televisions, stereos and other necessary graveyard items.
C. Some people will be dissatisfied no matter how much they have. They may want more, or they may want to keep what they have forever. One recent television documentary showed several people, motivated by boredom, jetting from New York to Paris for a one-day shopping spree to buy platinum earrings. In Brazil, some people are ordering coffins equipped with deluxe stereos, televisions and other graveyard necessities. The minimum price for these coffins—$45,000.
D. Some people are never satisfied. No matter how much they have they still want more, or think they can keep what they have forever. One television documentary recently showed several people flying from New York to Paris for the day to buy platinum earrings because they were bored. In Brazil, some people are ordering coffins that cost $45,000 and are equipped with deluxe stereos, televisions and other graveyard necessities.

9 (#2)

10.
I. A television signal or video signal has three parts.
II. Its parts are the black-and-white portion, the color portion, and the synchronizing (sync) pulses, which keep the picture stable.
III. Each video source, whether it's a camera or a video-cassette recorder contains its own generator of these synchronizing pulses to accompany the picture that it's sending in order to keep it steady and straight.
IV. In order to produce a clean recording, a video-cassette recorder must "lock-up" to the sync pulses that are part of the video it is trying to record, and this effort may be very noticeable if the device does not have gunlock.

10.____

   A. There are three parts to a television or video signal: the black-and-white part, the color part, and the synchronizing (sync) pulses, which keep the picture stable. Whether it's a video-cassette recorder or a camera, each video source contains its own pulse that synchronizes and generates the picture it's sending in order to keep it straight and steady. A video-cassette recorder must "lock up" to the sync pulses that are part of the video it's trying to record. If the device doesn't have gunlock, this effort must be very noticeable.
   B. A video signal or television is comprised of three parts: the black-and-white portion, the color portion, and the sync (synchronizing) pulses, which keep the picture stable. Whether it's a camera or a video-cassette recorder, each video source contains its own generator of these synchronizing pulses. These accompany the picture that it's sending in order to keep it straight and steady. A video-cassette recorder must "lock up" to the sync pulses that are part of the video it is trying to record in order to produce a clean recording. This effort may be very noticeable if the device does not have gunlock.
   C. There are three parts to a television or video signal: the color portion, the black-and-white portion, and the sync (synchronizing pulses). These keep the picture stable. Each video source, whether it's a video-cassette recorder or a camera, generates these synchronizing pulses accompanying the picture it's sending in order to keep it straight and steady. If a clean recording is to be produced, a video-cassette recorder must store the sync pulses that are part of the video it is trying to record. This effort may not be noticeable if the device does not have gunlock.
   D. A television signal or video signal has three parts: the black-and-white portion, the color portion, and the synchronizing (sync) pulses. It's the sync pulses which keep the picture stable, which accompany it and keep it steady and straight. Whether it's a camera or a video-cassette recorder, each video source contains its own generator of these synchronizing pulses. To produce a clean recording, a video-cassette recorder must "lock up" to the sync pulses that are part of the video it is trying to record. If the device does not have gunlock, this effort may be very noticeable.

KEY (CORRECT ANSWERS)

1. C
2. B
3. A
4. B
5. D

6. A
7. B
8. D
9. C
10. D

PREPARING WRITTEN MATERIAL
EXAMINATION SECTION
TEST 1

DIRECTIONS: Each question consists of a sentence which may or may not be an example of good English usage. Examine each sentence, considering grammar, punctuation, spelling, capitalization, and awkwardness. Then choose the correct statement about it from the four choices below it. If the English usage in the sentence given is better than any of the changes suggested in choices B, C, or D, pick choice A. (Do not pick a choice that will change the meaning of the sentence.) *PRINT THE LETTER OF THE CORRECT ANSWER IN THE SPACE AT THE RIGHT.*

1. We attended a staff conference on Wednesday the new safety and fire rules were discussed.   1.____
    - A. This is an example of acceptable writing.
    - B. The words "safety," "fire," and "rules" should begin with capital letters.
    - C. There should be a comma after the word "Wednesday."
    - D. There should be a period after the word "Wednesday" and the word "the" should begin with a capital letter.

2. Neither the dictionary or the telephone directory could be found in the office library.   2.____
    - A. This is an example of acceptable writing.
    - B. The word "or" should be changed to "nor."
    - C. The word "library" should be spelled "libery."
    - D. The word "neither" should be changed to "either."

3. The report would have been typed correctly if the typist could read the draft.   3.____
    - A. This is an example of acceptable writing.
    - B. The word "would" should be removed.
    - C. The word "have" should be inserted after the word "could."
    - D. The word "correctly" should be changed to "correct."

4. The supervisor brought the reports and forms to an employees desk.   4.____
    - A. This is an example of acceptable writing.
    - B. The word "brought" should be changed to "took."
    - C. There should be a comma after the word "reports" and a comma after the word "forms."
    - D. The word "employees" should be spelled "employee's."

5. It's important for all the office personnel to submit their vacation schedules on time.   5.____
    - A. This is an example of acceptable writing.
    - B. The word "It's" should be spelled "Its."
    - C. The word "their" should be spelled "they're."
    - D. The word "personnel" should be spelled "personal."

157

6. The report, along with the accompanying documents, were submitted for review.
   A. This is an example of acceptable writing.
   B. The words "were submitted" should be changed to "was submitted."
   C. The word "accompanying" should be spelled "accompaning."
   D. The comma after the word "report" should be taken out.

7. If others must use your files, be certain that they understand how the system works, but insist that you do all the filing and refiling.
   A. This is an example of acceptable writing.
   B. There should be a period after the word "works," and the word "but" should start a new sentence.
   C. The words "filing" and "refiling" should be spelled "fileing" and "refileing."
   D. There should be a comma after the word "but."

8. The appeal was not considered because of its late arrival.
   A. This is an example of acceptable writing.
   B. The word "its" should be changed to "it's."
   C. The word "its" should be changed to "the."
   D. The words "late arrival" should be changed to "arrival late."

9. The letter must be read carefuly to determine under which subject it should be filed.
   A. This is an example of acceptable writing.
   B. The word "under" should be changed to "at."
   C. The word "determine" should be spelled "determin."
   D. The word "carefuly" should be spelled "carefully."

10. He showed potential as an office manager, but he lacked skill in delegating work.
    A. This is an example of acceptable writing.
    B. The word "delegating" should be spelled "delagating."
    C. The word "potential" should be spelled "potencial."
    D. The words "he lacked" should be changed to "was lacking."

KEY (CORRECT ANSWERS)

1.	D	6.	B
2.	B	7.	A
3.	C	8.	A
4.	D	9.	D
5.	A	10.	A

TEST 2

DIRECTIONS: Each question consists of a sentence which may or may not be an example of good English usage. Examine each sentence, considering grammar, punctuation, spelling, capitalization, and awkwardness. Then choose the correct statement about it from the four choices below it. If the English usage in the sentence given is better than any of the changes suggested in choices B, C, or D, pick choice A. (Do not pick a choice that will change the meaning of the sentence.) *PRINT THE LETTER OF THE CORRECT ANSWER IN THE SPACE AT THE RIGHT.*

1. The supervisor wants that all staff members report to the office at 9:00 A.M.
   A. This is an example of acceptable writing.
   B. The word "that" should be removed and the word "to" should be inserted after the word "members."
   C. There should be a comma after the word "wants" and a comma after the word "office."
   D. The word "wants" should be changed to "want" and the word "shall" should be inserted after the word "members."

2. Every morning the clerk opens the office mail and distributes it.
   A. This is an example of acceptable writing.
   B. The word "opens" should be changed to "open."
   C. The word "mail" should be changed to "letters."
   D. The word "it" should be changed to "them."

3. The secretary typed more fast on a desktop computer than on a laptop computer.
   A. This is an example of acceptable writing.
   B. The words "more fast" should be changed to "faster."
   C. There should be a comma after the words "desktop computer."
   D. The word "than" should be changed to "then."

4. The new stenographer needed a desk a computer, a chair and a blotter.
   A. This is an example of acceptable writing.
   B. The word "blotter" should be spelled "blodder."
   C. The word "stenographer" should begin with a capital letter.
   D. There should be a comma after the word "desk."

5. The recruiting officer said, "There are many different goverment jobs available."
   A. This is an example of acceptable writing.
   B. The word "There" should not be capitalized.
   C. The word "government" should be spelled "government."
   D. The comma after the word "said" should be removed.

6. He can recommend a mechanic whose work is reliable.
   A. This is an example of acceptable writing.
   B. The word "reliable" should be spelled "relyable."
   C. The word "whose" should be spelled "who's."
   D. The word "mechanic should be spelled "mecanic."

7. She typed quickly; like someone who had not a moment to lose. 7._____
    A. This is an example of acceptable writing.
    B. The word "not" should be removed.
    C. The semicolon should be changed to a comma.
    D. The word "quickly" should be placed before instead of after the word "typed."

8. She insisted that she had to much work to do. 8._____
    A. This is an example of acceptable writing.
    B. The word "insisted" should be spelled "incisted."
    C. The word "to" used in front of "much" should be spelled "too."
    D. The word "do" should be changed to "be done."

9. He excepted praise from his supervisor for a job well done. 9._____
    A. This is an example of acceptable writing.
    B. The word "excepted" should be spelled "accepted."
    C. The order of the words "well done" should be changed to "done well."
    D. There should be a comma after the word "supervisor."

10. What appears to be intentional errors in grammar occur several times in the passage. 10._____
    A. This is an example of acceptable writing.
    B. The word "occur" should be spelled "occurr."
    C. The word "appears" should be changed to "appear."
    D. The phrase "several times" should be changed to "from time to time."

KEY (CORRECT ANSWERS)

1.	B		6.	A
2.	A		7.	C
3.	B		8.	C
4.	D		9.	B
5.	C		10.	C

TEST 3

DIRECTIONS: Each question consists of a sentence which may or may not be an example of good English usage. Examine each sentence, considering grammar, punctuation, spelling, capitalization, and awkwardness. Then choose the correct statement about it from the four choices below it. If the English usage in the sentence given is better than any of the changes suggested in choices B, C, or D, pick choice A. (Do not pick a choice that will change the meaning of the sentence.) *PRINT THE LETTER OF THE CORRECT ANSWER IN THE SPACE AT THE RIGHT.*

1. The clerk could have completed the assignment on time if he knows where these materials were located.
    A. This is an example of acceptable writing.
    B. The word "knows" should be replaced by "had known."
    C. The word "were" should be replaced by "had been."
    D. The words "where these materials were located" should be replaced by "the location of these materials."

2. All employees should be given safety training. Not just those who accidents.
    A. This is an example of acceptable writing.
    B. The period after the word "training" should be changed to a colon.
    C. The period after the word "training" should be changed to a semicolon, and the first letter of the word "Not" should be changed to a small "n."
    D. The period after the word "training" should be changed to a comma, and the first letter of the word "Not" should be changed to a small "n."

3. This proposal is designed to promote employee awareness of the suggestion program, to encourage employee participation in the program, and to increase the number of suggestions submitted.
    A. This is an example of acceptable writing.
    B. The word "proposal" should be spelled "proposal."
    C. The words "to increase the number of suggestions submitted" should be changed to "an increase in the number of suggestions is expected."
    D. The word "promote" should be changed to "enhance" and the word "increase" should be changed to "add to."

4. The introduction of inovative managerial techniques should be preceded by careful analysis of the specific circumstances and conditions in each department.
    A. This is an example of acceptable writing.
    B. The word "technique" should be spelled "techneques."
    C. The word "inovative" should be spelled "innovative."
    D. A comma should be placed after the word "circumstances" and after the word "conditions."

5. This occurrence indicates that such criticism embarrasses him.   5.____
    A. This is an example of acceptable writing.
    B. The word "occurrence" should be spelled "occurence."
    C. The word "criticism" should be spelled "critisism.
    D. The word "embarrasses" should be spelled "embarasses.

KEY (CORRECT ANSWERS)

1. B
2. D
3. A
4. C
5. A

www.ingramcontent.com/pod-product-compliance
Lightning Source LLC
Chambersburg PA
CBHW081819300426
44116CB00014B/2415